Gospel Living

Gospel Living:

Applying the Gospel to Life Until it Becomes a Lifestyle

Jonathan Kyle

Copyright© 2021 Jonathan Kyle
All rights reserved.

Paperback ISBN: 978-0-578-32138-7

All Quotes from Scripture (unless otherwise noted) are taken from *The Holy Bible English Standard Version.* Copyright 2000, 2001 by Crossway Bibles, a division of Good News Publishers.

Scripture quotations marked NIV are taken from the *Holy Bible, New International Version.* NIV. Copyright 1973, 1978, 1984 by International Bible Society.

Dedication

This book is dedicated to my wife, Amanda who has been so instrumental by God to help me learn the very realities of applying the Gospel to life until it becomes a lifestyle. She embodies so many of these gospel aspects to a greater degree than I could even aspire to possess. It is also dedicated to my four kids with whom God uses to remind me to practice what I preach on a day-to-day basis. They are a joy to watch grow up and wrestle with the truths of God's Word. May this book be a lasting reminder to you of how your dad desired to live before the Lord.

CONTENTS

Acknowledgements   *i*

Introduction   *vi*

The Gospel and a Warning   *1*

Gospel Lifestyle-Love and Justice   *32*

Gospel Lifestyle-Grace   *56*

Gospel Lifestyle-Mercy and Forgiveness   *72*

Gospel Lifestyle-Humility and Service   *89*

Gospel Lifestyle-Peace and Patience   *110*

Gospel Living-Endurance, Holiness, and Joy   *137*

Concluding Thoughts   *156*

Acknowledgements

You might ask, "Why are you even writing this book?". That is a great question, and the only response that I can think of is that in my experience in full time ministry, I have realized that no truth that I preach from God's Word is new. In fact, the message that has been preached from orthodoxy over the past 2,000 years has never and will never change. However, there is still the need for pastors, teachers, communicators, and evangelists to speak eternal truths then, now, and forevermore. The reason is because while the truth never changes, the way truth is communicated constantly changes from culture to culture and generation to generation. The way the truth of the Bible was communicated 50 years ago by gifted communicators and pastors may not be understood by a current 13-year-old boy who lives in a world of iPads, video games, and social media.

Furthermore, people in general have a hard time retaining information we hear throughout any given day. But if we hear a story, a well-crafted question, or a proposed problem that relates to our current situation, our ears perk up, and we subconsciously tell ourselves to store away the information that we are about to hear in our memory bank for current or future use. Countless are the times that I have personally read a familiar Scripture and the truth that was dormant for a number of years, now, jumps off of the page because of a circumstance that God has brought, or is bringing, me through. Additionally, there have been multiple times that students and adults have approached me after a message to express their same amazement at a truth that was hiding in plain sight and that had somehow evaded them to that point. As a pastor, I know that I did not reveal that truth to them but it was the work of the Holy Spirit in illumination. I also know that God uses the stories and illustrations of a pastor to serve as connecting points for the hearers to understand truth. So pastors, teachers, evangelists, communicators, or Christians in general throughout all of history will continue to repeat the time tested truth of God's Word in different ways until Christ's Second Coming.

Therefore, I write this book not to unveil new life-changing truth from God's

Word but to communicate the never-changing truth of God in a different way so that for the first (or umpteenth time) you read it you will understand it, believe it to be true, and apply it to your life until God's Word becomes a lifestyle.

    This work could not be possible without the co-laboring of my wife Amanda in the ministry who is tirelessly taking care of our four gifts from God: Corban, Jadon, Kyson, and Livia. She puts in more hours than I do by feeding, schooling, and taking care of the basic needs of our kids, while serving in the student ministry, and discipling young ladies.

    Thanks to my parents for all your support and prayer throughout the years, and thanks to my brother and sister-in-law, Jamie and Kelli, for living out the Gospel by starting a nonprofit organization to reach out to those who are hurting. A special thanks to Jamie to continually encouraging me to keep pressing on throughout my life.

    I am grateful to my student pastors, Stan and Mike, who took a loving interest in me and made a huge investment in discipling me, which is paying off in huge blessings in my life. Thanks to my former pastor Jamie for his faithfulness to preach the truth in many different ways so that my stubborn heart would finally hear and understand, but, most of all, for living out his faith so evidently in front of me and the church.

Finally, thanks to my friends and church family for the countless conversations about some of the very topics that are in this book, but also for their love and concern for me and my family. I want to say "Thank you" again to my church family for providing me with a sabbatical, which has given me the time to write this book. To God be the glory for all things that He has, is, and will do through the investment the church has made in my life.

v

Introduction

As a sports enthusiast, I know the importance of practice in one particular sport. There are a couple of key aspects, among many others, that an athlete seeks to accomplish in practice. Muscle memory and the ability to read and react are some of the most basic elements. Let me explain these terms as I understand them. Muscle memory is the replication of a certain movement to the point that an athlete can duplicate this motion subconsciously or as you might say "with their eyes closed." Some of the best jump shooters in the NBA can line up with the goal, close their eyes, go through their shooting motion, and make the shot. They accomplish the task because of the thousands, possibly millions, of shots they have practiced over their lifetime. Muscle memory creates the ability for the athlete to perform a task almost subconsciously, which may be similar to you or me walking and chewing gum at the same time. Repetition plays a key role in our lives.

In order to get better at reading and reacting, the best drills to run in a practice setting are the ones that duplicate a possible scenario that the athlete may encounter during a game. A coach will set up a certain scenario to teach the player to process what they are seeing in order to analyze, determine, and evaluate what their desired reaction should be. This is very similar to how a child learns to read. They familiarize themselves with the letters and even words, so that when they see the words, they read, comprehend, and speak them all at the same time. In the same way, the coach hopes that through enough repetition the player will process the information being received and respond automatically without thinking.

This experience brought me to a point of spiritual decision when I was in the 8th grade. I was saved at the age of seven but did not progress much as a believer until I entered the student ministry at my church in the 7th grade. There I learned the importance of spending time alone with God in His Word and how to have a quiet time. My spiritual walk began to increase greatly as I took God's Word at face value by putting it into practice. However, I began to notice a lot of discrepancies between my life and the will of God spelled out in His Word. I managed these discrepancies by being aware of who was around me and behaving like a dutiful

Christian when my student pastor, Sunday School teacher, or parents were around. But after a while this became nerve-racking and tiring due to constantly having to be aware of my surroundings. One morning while walking to church from my friend's house I became aware of the mask I was wearing. It was then that I became ready to lay down my hypocrisy at Christ's feet. I was tired of living a double life around certain people. That day I told God I wanted to be the same person all the time no matter who was around me, and the person I wanted to be was the one whom God called me to be in His Word.

Perhaps, that is why my favorite verse in high school was James 1:22, "Do not merely listen to the word, and so deceive yourselves. Do what it says" (NIV). I learned that my intellectual knowledge about Bible stories did not make me a better Christian. Therefore, I wanted to take God's Word and apply it to my life until it became a lifestyle.

Remember the sports illustration from above, repetition is necessary in our lives to bring about the Christ exalting lives that God has called us to in knowing Him and making Him known. That means that each Christian should take the Word of God, read it, and immediately begin to discover how they can apply that truth to their lives and then go and do it. That may look like playing a possible scenario in your head and concluding how you will respond, so that when something similar takes place in real life then you will know what to do. In other words, "read and react."

My intent in writing this book is to blend two deep passions of mine: the Gospel, and the application of God's Word to our lives. The Gospel stands as the single most important motivation to a Christian's life. A Christian should want to know more about God while at the same time applying the truths about God to his life, so others may know who He is and what He has done for them.

In no way am I advocating the practice of Gospel and biblical principles to earn favor with God. Nor am I saying that adding Gospel characteristics to your life will bring you salvation. If our lives have been drastically changed by the Gospel of Jesus Christ and His work on the cross, then the resulting changes should cause us to look like the very One who saved us.

The Gospel should serve as the very reason why we do what we do: we love others, help those in need, forgive someone of a wrong they have done to us, show grace through a second chance, reconcile broken relationships, reach out to the outcast, and the list goes on and on. So, read through this book, and bask in the glory of the Gospel. May it lead you to apply Christlike attributes to your life until those attributes shape the way you live.

"Our lives should look like the very Gospel that changed us."

Chapter 1:

The Gospel and a Warning

"for [THE GOSPEL] is the power of God for salvation to everyone who believes…"
Romans 1:16

What is the Gospel?

The Gospel message is essential to the Christian faith. Without it, there is no hope, no joy, no peace, and really, no life. The Good News itself is the linchpin between knowledge of God and the practical nature of our faith. If we have no understanding of the doctrine (an agreed upon set of beliefs) of God, Jesus, and humanity, then we don't see our need for the Gospel. If we have all the knowledge of these doctrines and lack the fruits of this knowledge, then there is no redemption or transformation.

These two sides of the Gospel knowledge and fruits are necessary to keep in mind as we seek to understand what the Gospel is and live it out in our lives. In our desire to make the definition of the Gospel short, concise, and easy to repeat we must not shortchange it to be something that it is not. Nor should we make the Gospel all about "getting to go to heaven." When we do this we can confuse people into believing something they did not fully understand and subsequently live lives that are stunted in growth, if there is any life there at all. Let's do away with gospel definitions like "God loves you and has a wonderful plan for your life" or ones that do not give us a full understanding of our need like "God will forgive you of your sins if you believe in Him." That is an essential truth of the Gospel, but some people do not know why they need to be forgiven of their sins or even what "sin" is. Instead, we must be clear to state *who* God is, while simultaneously stating *what* He has done, and *how* a person receives this truly good news. The implications of the Gospel on a person's life will then flow out of the *who, what*, and *how* of the Gospel message.

The definition that I propose to you in this book is a definition composed by David Delmotte, a pastor and friend whom I served alongside for the sake of the Gospel. His definition of the Gospel is:

Gospel Living

"The Holy, Loving, Creator God, confronted with human hostility and rebellion has chosen in His Own freedom and faithfulness, to become Redeemer and Restorer of man to God and God's purposes made possible by grace, through faith and surrender in the crucified and risen King, Jesus Christ."

This definition can easily be broken into four parts which we will explore with greater detail and understanding; 1) God, 2) Man, 3) Jesus, and 4) Surrender.

God-The Holy Loving Creator God

This may seem obvious to some, but the Bible is about God and written for us. God's glory is what drives the universe and brought it into being through the power of His spoken Word. And His glory is what sustains the universe.[1] We understand this in the first few verses in John 1:1-4 that say, "*In the beginning was the Word, and the Word was with God, and the Word was God. He was in the beginning with God. All things were made through him, and without him was not anything made that was made. In him was life and the life was the light of men.*"

Here we gather that God has always existed and simultaneously the Son has always existed. God has existed for all

---

[1] Matt Chandler & Jared Wilson, "The Explicit Gospel," (Wheaton, IL: Crossway, 2012), 34-35.

eternity past and will exist for eternity future. There is no beginning or end to God... "He is." We see in verse 3 that God the Father is the One who made all things through Jesus. In God, there is life and that life is revealed through the Son because they are one. And all of creation knows who God is because the Son, who is the true light, has made the truth about God known to the world. This revealing of God more clearly through God Incarnate, Jesus Christ, is similar to when God created the light and revealed creation out of the darkness.[2]

John Piper says, "The further up you go in the revealed thoughts of God, the clearer you see that God's aim in creating the world was to display the value of His own glory."[3] So God created all things to display His glory. Even the creation itself proclaims the glory of God as Psalm 19:1 tells us, "*The heavens declare the glory of God and the skies proclaim the works of His hands.*" Christians know that we were all created to display His glory. The Westminster Shorter Catechism tells us, "The chief end of man is to glorify God, and to enjoy Him forever." [4] The conclusion is that all human beings are created to acknowledge, submit to, and enjoy the supremacy of God in all things.

---

[2] "The ESV Study Bible, English Standard Version," (Wheaton, IL: Crossway, 2008), 2019.

[3] John Piper, "God's Passion for His Glory: Living the Vision of Jonathan Edwards," (Wheaton, IL: Crossway, 1998), 32.

[4] "Westminster Shorter Catechism," 1st ed. 1011, Q1.

They are to ascribe to Him the glory and praise that He deserves. And the enjoyment of it is displayed through worship.[5]

But you and I are allergic to the idea that everything, including us, exists not for ourselves but for the glory of God.[6] We see that in verse 10 of John 1 when the Bible says, "*He [Christ] was in the world, and the world was made through Him, yet the world did not know Him.*" We read there that God created all things through the Son, and the Son reveals to the world that God is Creator. But the world (you and I) chooses to ignore Him and not to know Him.

This is like copyright infringement. Copyright laws protect the original works of the author, so they receive the proper recognition and rewards for their music, movie, drama, or book. The laws guard against someone else claiming it as their own. The laws do allow for certain permissions to be given to others to use the author's original work in some fashion but almost always for some kind of royalty or payment and written agreement as to how the material will be used. This makes perfect sense because the author has every right of authority over their work of art, and there are harsh penalties for anyone who violates the agreement or law such as a $250,000 fine and five years in prison.

---

[5] Matt Chandler & Jared Wilson, "The Explicit Gospel," (Wheaton, IL: Crossway, 2012), 36
[6] Ibid., 34

Jonathan Kyle

In essence, every human who does not submit to the Lordship of God is breaking His copyright laws. God created every human being in His image to display His glory. Every time we as humans choose to reject God's expectations on our lives, then we are not living according to our intended use and are invoking a penalty upon ourselves.

Because God created us, we are responsible to Him and to the expectations that He has laid out for us in Scripture. Greg Gilbert sums up this thought in his book *What is the Gospel* when he writes, "Despite our constant talk and liberty, we are not as free as we would like to think. We are created. We are made. Therefore, we are owned." I like to explain this idea to people with an illustration. Imagine that I have just created a brand-new board game called "Bumfuzzled" (this is a word we use in the south to mean confused). Since I created this game, I possess the right to make up the rules of the game. The reason "why" is that I know the purpose for which I designed it and the rules that need to be in place to make it enjoyable and reach its intended end. No one looks at me and says my rules are unfair, too restricting, or do not make sense. Why? Because I created this game and know how it works best. You can create your own rules if you would like, but you will never reach my desired end as the creator of the game.

In the same way, God created the world and everything in it, including you and me. God has His desired end in mind, and the best way to navigate through this life is spelled out in His Word. That is not to say that everything will be perfect, but He has graciously made known to His creation His intended purpose and the way to reach that purpose. We are not left to blindly navigate through this life hoping to reach the Creator's designed purpose.

What does our Creator expect from us? This can be summed up in Leviticus 19:2. It says, *"...You shall be holy, for I the Lord your God am holy."* The book of Leviticus describes through more than 600 laws, how God's people can be holy, set apart and pure. Jesus makes it really easy for us though and sums it up in two laws, *"...love the Lord your God with all your heart and with all your soul, and with all your mind...And a second is like it: You shall love your neighbor as yourself"* (Matthew 22:37, 39). With these expectations of holiness, we have a big cause for concern for all of humanity because James tells us in 2:10, *"For whoever keeps the whole law and yet stumbles at just one point is guilty of breaking all of it"* (NIV). The conclusion: God created all of humanity; humanity is responsible to God and His expectations; and His expectation is perfection.

Jonathan Kyle

Man-Confronted with human hostility and rebellion

Francis Schaeffer, a contemporary theologian, was once asked that if he had one hour on a train with a lost man, how much time would he give to each section of the Gospel message. He responded by saying, "I would spend 45-50 minutes on the negative, to really show him his dilemma—that he is morally dead—then I'd take 10-15 minutes to preach the Gospel."[7] You really do not know how much you need something until you see the desperate condition that you are in. This is what advertising agencies base their whole appeal on. They are trying to set up a scenario in their ad in which you can see how much easier life would be if you bought their product.

The same is true for people and their need for the Gospel. The United States has changed over the past 50-70 years in regard to people's biblical literacy. Walking up to someone on the street and telling them "You are a sinner who needs to be forgiven of their sins" was a phrase that most people used to understand. However, today not only will people be blown away by your abrupt confrontation, they may not believe they are a bad person or that sin even exists. The common belief today is that man is basically

---
[7] Will Metzger, "Tell the Truth: The Whole Gospel to the Whole Person by Whole People," (Downers Grove, IL: Intervarsity Press, 1981), 61.

good. But the question is "what is our standard of good?".

I love the game of football and I have been a fan for as long as I can remember. I even had the privilege of playing football when I was younger. I would consider myself a pretty good football player and have several awards to show for it. However, the assumption that I am a pretty good football player is subjectively based upon the standard of competition that I faced. When I tell you that my football experience is limited to pee wee, high school, and backyard football, then you come to a quick conclusion that the standard I am comparing myself to is not very high. The reality is I could have never played for a Division 1 college or even dreamed about playing for the NFL. My standard of comparison is too low.

The standard that most people have for themselves in deciding whether or not they are a good person is very low as well. For most, their standard is being a better person than Adolf Hitler or Joseph Stalin. For others, they compare themselves to a neighbor down the street who they know has done something bad. (Is it not odd that we usually compare ourselves to people we know have issues and not to someone who is morally better than us?) The problem is that none of these people is the standard. The standard is perfection which we looked at above. And if you think reading through the Levitical law is too hard to gain an understanding of God's Holiness, then just look at Jesus' life because He set the standard as well. Peter tells us that in 1 Peter 1:15, *"as he who called you is holy, you also be holy in all your conduct."*

The reality is that mankind has rebelled against God and is, at core, a sinner. Every last individual on this earth has sinned. With an honest evaluation of our lives, it would not take long for us to realize this is true. First of all, the Bible tells us in Romans 3:23 when the Word says, *"for all have sinned and fall short of the glory of God."* Second, one can take a quick look at the 10 Commandments and discover that they have been guilty of breaking at least one of those commands once in their lifetime. If we remember the passage from James 2:10, *"For whoever keeps the whole law and yet stumbles at just one point is guilty of breaking all of it"* (NIV), we can conclude that we are guilty of breaking all of the law of God.

Some people complain that keeping the entire 600 and something laws is just unfair. I want to remind you that there were not always 600 plus laws, but at one point there was only ONE negative (there was the command to "be fruitful and multiply and fill the earth and subdue it...") law to obey. In Genesis 2:16-17, God told Adam, *"You may surely eat of every tree of the garden, but of the tree of the knowledge of good and evil you shall not eat, for in the day that you eat of it you shall surely die."* In the very next chapter in verse 6 the Bible says, *"the woman saw that the tree was good for food, and that it was a delight to the eyes, and that the tree was to be desired to make one wise, she took of its fruit and ate, and she also gave some to her husband who was with her, and he ate."* ONE RULE!

Adam and Eve messed up because they wanted to be like God. Is that not what is at the heart of all our sin or disobedience? We want to be like God and to decide what is right and what is wrong. We want autonomy. We want self-governance. The Bible tells us specifically that every human who ever walks this earth is at their core a sinner as a result of our first ancestor Adam. Romans 5:12 says, *"Therefore, just as sin came into the world through one man, and death through sin, and so death spread to all men because all sinned."*

We could respond and say, "That was Adam and Eve and they are responsible for their own sin." Well, yes and no. They were responsible for their sin and were punished in several ways, but two significant ways affect you, me, and everyone else. First, they were driven out of the Garden resulting in the loss of their intimate relationship they had with God (vs. 23). Second, they would physically die (vs. 19). While there are other effects of sin like our work being extremely difficult, extreme pain in childbirth, and physically dying, the most significant and eternal effect is that everyone has been separated from God for all eternity. I believe Isaiah describes this effect best when he is talking to the Israelites in Isaiah 59:2. He says, "*but your iniquities have made a SEPARATION* (emphasis mine) *between you and your God, and your sins have HIDDEN his face from you so that he does not hear.*"

The overarching problem that all of humanity has is that there is absolutely nothing we can do to make our relationship with God good again. Some people think that being a good person or even keeping the Law will grant them the privilege of communing with God again. But Paul tells us the intent of the Law in Romans 3:20 when he says, "*through the law comes knowledge of sin.*" In other words, the Law was never given as a way to gain salvation but to reveal the NEED for salvation. Isaiah laments this despair of the effects of sin in 64:5 and says, "*Shall we be saved?*" He realizes their helpless situation when he says, "*all our righteous deeds are like a polluted garment.*" His best day, and ours, is not good enough to gain back our relationship with God. Instead, our best day of "works" is appalling and disgusting to God. We are desperately in need of great help! The conclusion: Man is not good. At his core he is a rebellious sinner separated from God with no hope in his ability to reconcile that relationship.

Gospel Living

Jesus-has chosen in His Own freedom to become Redeemer and Restorer

This section is the proverbial "sweet spot" of the Gospel for it is the "Good News" for all of humanity. As we have just seen, mankind is in a desperate situation. We are not able to meet the standard of perfection that God has given us. On top of that, sin has brought upon us the deserved wrath of God for our willful disobedience. We, as humans, have taken what God has designed and hijacked it as our own. We now await the dreadful punishment of God for sin which is eternal death and separation from Him. In recognizing our wretched condition, we echo the words of Paul as he understands his sinful condition and says, *"Who will deliver me from this body of death?" (Romans 7:24).*

The sweet answer is found in the very next verse. When Paul has come to the most dismal of all conclusions, that we are wretched individuals who do the very sinful things that we say we are not going to do, I imagine he shouts these words as he writes, *"Thanks be to God through Jesus Christ our Lord!"* (vs. 25) It is Jesus Christ who can save us from our hopeless situation of sin, death, and destruction. The Son of God, Jesus, takes on human flesh and dwells among us. Jesus humbly submits His life to the will of the Father and NEVER sins. He is wrongfully accused and is sentenced to death on the cross. He dies and is buried in a borrowed tomb. Three days later He rises from the grave then appears to the disciples and more than 500 other people. For those of you who have grown up in the church, you may know why all of those details are significant. But to those of you who are new to the faith or have never heard the Gospel, then you do not understand why any of those details are significant or even helpful in granting you forgiveness of your sins and the removal of your guilty verdict. Once again, we need a clear understanding of the entirety of Scripture to see why Jesus' life, death, burial, and resurrection are capable of removing the sins of the world.

While Genesis 3 contains what is called "The Fall," or the first sin of mankind that brought about separation, death, and destruction, there is a glimpse of hope that exists amidst the punishment that God gave as a result of sin. In verse 15 of chapter 3, God is handing out the punishment to the serpent, and God says, *"I will put enmity between you and the woman, and between your offspring and her offspring; he shall bruise your head, and you shall bruise his heel."* Here, God is promising the redemption of mankind through the offspring of Eve (Jesus) who will crush the head of the serpent, Satan. Throughout the rest of the Old Testament we continually see messages of hope and redemption that point to God making all things new and right again which will come through the promised Messiah.

Gospel Living

One of the greatest events of the Old Testament that helps us understand Christ and His sacrifice is the Passover. The Jews, who are God's chosen people, have been enslaved by the Egyptians for 400 years. God has heard the cries of His people and has seen their mistreatment, and He has raised up Moses as His instrument of grace to deliver His people out from under the mighty power of the Egyptian nation. Through tumultuous negotiations between Moses, Aaron (Moses' brother), and the Pharaoh of Egypt, the Pharaoh was shown many mighty works of God through nine different plagues that greatly affected Pharaoh and his people. While some of these plagues convinced Pharaoh to agree to let the Jews go, his heart would harden and he would refuse again to let God's people go. All of these events culminated in the tenth and final plague. It was the death of all the firstborn babies of the land. Unlike the previous nine plagues that did not affect the Jews, the tenth plague could affect them if they did not listen and obey the instruction of the Lord.

The Lord gave Moses and Aaron these instructions to give to the people of God in Exodus 12:

"Tell all the congregation of Israel that on the tenth day of this month every man shall take a lamb...Your lamb shall be without blemish, a male a year old...you shall keep it until the fourteenth day of this month, when

the whole assembly of the congregation of Israel shall kill their lambs at twilight. Then they shall take some of the blood and put it on the two doorposts and the lintel of the houses in which they eat it…In this manner you shall eat it; with your belt fastened, your sandals on your feet, and your staff in your hand. And you shall eat it in haste. It is the Lord's Passover. For I will pass through the land of Egypt that night, and I will strike all the firstborn in the land of Egypt…The blood shall be a sign for you, on the houses where you are. And when I see the blood, I will pass over you, and no plague will befall you to destroy you, when I strike the land of Egypt." (12:3, 5-7, 11-13)

What we see in this instruction is that God made a way for a "spotless lamb" to die in the place of the firstborn children who lived in each home. This is a doctrine called "substitutionary atonement." This means that the payment required by God (the death of the firstborn) was satisfied by a substitute, in this case, a "spotless lamb." Through this event in the redemptive history of the Scriptures, we can understand why Jesus' death on the cross can serve as the payment for someone's sin. We can say this with confidence because Jesus, Himself, said it in Mark 10:45, "*For even the Son of Man came not to be served but to serve, and to give his life as a ransom for many.*" If His own proclamations as substitute for many were not clear enough, there are other authors in Scripture who said the very same thing. Peter says, "*For Christ also suffered once for sins, THE RIGHTEOUS FOR THE UNRIGHTEOUS* (emphasis mine)*, that he might BRING US TO GOD, being put to death in the flesh but made alive in the spirit*" (1 Peter 3:18). God makes it clear throughout Scripture that "substitutionary atonement" is the only viable way to bring about the reconciliation of sinners to Himself.

It would be an understatement to say that I love super heroes! The super hero plays on the desire of young boys to do things that are beyond their limits to help someone else that is in need. There was not a day that went by, when I was young and outside playing, that I was not pretending to save the day. But have you ever noticed that superheroes' powers are typically suited just right for the task they need to accomplish and for the environment in which they are placed? As an example, take Spiderman and put him in a small rural town where there are more fields than there are tall buildings. Spidey would be arriving to save the day on his Spideybike more than swinging in from the rooftops. But put Spiderman in a big city, and he can get around quickly to save the day. Or do you not find it convenient that the brains of Batman are coupled with his limitless resources. Take his riches away and he has about the same ability as you and me to change the crime rates in our cities.

While these superheroes are fictional, Jesus is the God-Man who is perfectly suited by God to accomplish the task that was assigned to Him.

One of the ways that Jesus was perfectly suited to come and take away the sins of men is because He was and is sinless. First Peter 2:22 says, "*He committed no sin, neither was deceit found in his mouth.*" The Apostle John supports this truth in 1 John 3:5 when he penned under the inspiration of the Holy Spirit, "*You know that he appeared to take away sins, and in him there is no sin.*" Jesus was sinless and was the "spotless lamb" that was referred to at the Passover. But you have to ask yourself, why is that important? There are two important theological reasons and one very practical reason.

First, He was the perfect and acceptable sacrifice that was required by God. Just as we built the case above that everyone has fallen short of God's standard by being disobedient to His laws, we can also say that if one were to keep the standard of God (which no human could do) then they are a perfect person. As such, Jesus meets God's standard and can serve in the role as THE "spotless lamb" who can be the substitute for sinners.

Second, because Jesus was perfect and without sin, He had no need to make payment for His own sins. This was the problem with the OT system of worship and sacrifice. The priests who served as God's representative to man and man's representative to God were sinners themselves and needed to make payment for their own sins before offering sacrifices on behalf of others. Because of that, they could never offer themselves as substitutes for someone else because they did not meet the requirements of holiness to do so.

The very practical dimension of Jesus' sinlessness is a living and breathing model to follow. Peter tells us this in 1 Peter 1:15 when he says, *"as he who called you is holy, you also be holy in all your conduct."* If you want a real-life example of what it looks like to live in full submission to God, then look at the life of Christ and model your life around His.

The other reason that Jesus is perfectly suited to bring salvation to mankind is that He is both God and Man. There is great significance in the fact that God took on flesh in Jesus. The author of Hebrews rejoices in the fact that God dwelt among us and returned to heaven by saying, *"For we do not have a high priest who is unable to sympathize with our weaknesses, but one who in every respect has been tempted as we are, yet without sin. Let us then with confidence draw near to the throne of grace, that we may receive mercy and find grace to help in time of need"* (Heb. 4:15-16). By Jesus taking on flesh, He serves as our representative upon the cross.

His sacrifice is eternal! Unlike the animals who were offered over and over again for the sins of God's people, this was a once and for all sacrifice made by Jesus that lasts for all eternity. There will never be another need to offer anything or anyone else as a sacrifice because the sacrifice of Jesus is good for all eternity. IT IS FINISHED!

Now, we know why Jesus' sacrifice was important and how He was well suited for the task, but what did He actually do? The short answer is that Jesus took upon Himself the sins of the world and suffered the wrath of God for those sins that were upon Him. The wrath of God resulted in His death. Jesus' death and shedding of blood is important because Hebrews 9:22 says, *"without the shedding of blood there is no forgiveness of sins."* So, Jesus takes our sins upon Himself, receives the wrath of God that is deserved for every sinner, and provides for us a way to be forgiven of our sins. Why? Why would anyone do this?

Let us read Scripture and find that answer to the "why." Paul gives us this answer in Romans 5:7-8 when he says, *"For one will scarcely die for a righteous person—though perhaps for a good person one would dare even to die—BUT GOD SHOWS HIS LOVE FOR US in that while we were still sinners, Christ died for us."* It is God's amazing love that He has for His creation that moves Him to go to such great lengths to bring us back to Himself. You may have heard of this heartwarming truth in John 3:16 that says, "*For God so loved the world, that he gave his only Son, that whoever believes in him should not perish but have eternal life.*" God, in His love, has paved the way through His Son to make us righteous so that we might enjoy the relationship that we are made for with our Creator.

But Christ did not just die on the cross for our sins. In fact, if Jesus would have remained dead, then those who believe in Jesus "*are of all people most to be pitied*" (1 Cor. 15:19). And Jesus would be no more than a good man who died for His cause. But this is not the end because three days later Christ rose from the grave defeating sin, death, and the grave. His ability to defeat sin, death, and the grave reveals His power over sin and death. So "*thanks be to God, who gives us the victory through our Lord Jesus Christ*" (1 Cor. 15:57). In other words, no one has to suffer the consequences of sin, but can, through Christ, receive forgiveness and salvation. Conclusion: Christ serves as our spotless great high priest (representing God to man and man to God) who bore our sins and the wrath of God on Himself, defeating sin, death, and the grave, now reigning as deserving King who bestows His righteousness through grace on all who believe.

Surrender-made possible by grace through faith

Someone can know all of the truth that is mentioned above, but until they receive the Gospel to be true, it will never be effective in their life. As good as it might sound that the Gospel would just automatically save every person who ever walks the earth because of what Jesus did, the truth is that in God's holiness, sin cannot go unpunished in a person's life. Each individual needs to come to the understanding of his own sin, confess it before God, and ask for His forgiveness. In so doing, he is acknowledging the authority of God over his life and is giving Him the glory that He deserves. In other words, there is a response that every human being must have to the love of God that has been demonstrated through the giving of His one and only Son, Jesus.

In actuality, the offer of salvation is an amazing act of grace that does not have to be extended to anyone in God's creation. God, in no way, is obligated to save His creation that has rebelled against His authority and purpose. But God has chosen to extend grace to all of humanity to receive His salvation. Grace will be defined at greater length later in this book, but for the time being we will just say grace is receiving something that you do not deserve. So, God has given humanity grace by paving a way for His creation to be right with Him again through the substitutionary death of Jesus Christ.

Like any gift that is given to us, we must receive it. Oftentimes at Christmas, a gift is extended to us in a pretty packaging. We then physically reach out and take from the hands of the giver. In regard to receiving salvation, the grace given is extended to us through the Word of God and must be received by faith. Faith is not the idea of having confidence in something or someone. I often hear "faith" mentioned on the sidelines with football teams saying things like "I have faith in our quarterback to make the right decisions and play well." Or someone who seems to be giving themselves a pep talk about having faith that something is going to happen in their life. Or in politics, we have faith in this candidate to do the right thing. Not every time, but sometimes the quarterback makes a stupid decision, and it costs the team the game. Or the thing that the person has faith is going to happen does not, and the politician that you voted for lets you down. It is no wonder that the world often defines faith as "believing in something that we *hope* is real even though there is no proof of it."

Faith as defined by the Scripture is far from wishful thinking. God gives us His clear meaning of faith in Hebrews 11:1 when the Word says, "*Now faith is the ASSURANCE of things hoped for, the CONVICTION* (emphasis mine) *of things not seen."* The words "assurance" and "conviction" do not sound anything like "wish" or "aspiration." These words communicate confidence that what you believe by faith is as good as having already been done. That is the kind of faith that God calls us to have. The truth is that we could never muster up enough of this kind of faith to believe the Gospel that God has given us. Instead, that faith is given to us by God. Read this familiar text found in Ephesians 2:8-9 that says, *"For it is by grace that you have been saved, through faith, and this is NOT OF YOURSELF but a GIFT FROM GOD* (emphasis mine) *so that no one can boast."* I love what John Macarthur says, "When a person chokes or drowns and stops breathing, there is nothing he can do. If he ever breathes again, it will be because someone else starts him breathing. A person who is spiritually dead cannot even make a decision of faith unless God first breathes into him the breath of spiritual life. Faith is simply breathing the breath that God's grace supplies."[8] So while we might be able to give a response to all of the questions someone has about God, no one will ever make a genuine decision to place their faith in Jesus Christ as their Savior without the grace of God giving them the faith to believe the Gospel to be true. This is supported by what Jesus says in John 6:44, *"No one can come*

---

[8] John MacArthur, "Is Faith a Gift: Ephesians 2," *Grace to You* (December 17, 2015), http://www.gty.org/resources/bible-qna/BQ053113/is-faith-a-gift.

to me unless the Father who sent me DRAWS him..." We receive the Gospel by faith and that faith is given to us by God so that we have no reason to boast, thinking we saved ourselves. God has removed the possibility that we would receive the credit for our salvation. Instead, He causes us to continually give Him all the glory that He is due. When we place our faith in Christ, we are declaring that we have no hope in ourselves, our heart is not good at all, and we trust Christ alone for salvation.

Faith in Christ is often said to have a simultaneous action of repentance. Faith and repentance are not two separate things but are the flip sides of the same coin. You cannot have faith without repentance or repentance without faith. Repentance is the turning away from something and turning to something or someone else. When one turns away from their sin, they are at the same time turning to Christ in faith as their Savior. It is helpful to view faith and repentance as two sides of the same coin because we can be tempted to believe that if I turn away from my sin then in some way, I have gained my salvation. A person's repentance not only results in the change of their outward behavior but in the change of their attitude as well when they submit their desires to the desires of God.

There is a beautiful benefit that comes in knowing that when you receive the Gospel message, the forgiveness you receive is not a "work" you accomplished. If God has done the work of salvation in your life by giving you faith to believe, how could you undo something you have never done in the first place? In other words, if you have no ability to gain salvation, then you have no ability to undo what God has done for you in giving you salvation. He will keep you to the end! The conclusion: Salvation is not something that you earn but receive by faith and repentance as a free gift when you surrender to the love of God.

A Warning

I cringe at the thought of writing a book like this that is so practical in nature because of the potential backlash from people who don't take the time to read carefully through it. From the outside looking in, this book can appear to be just another self-help Christian book that is bent on modifying the behavior of Christians without giving them the sustenance of the Scripture which is needed to undergird and motivate the very reason we strive to live a different life.

The warning I am giving each reader is not to substitute the responsibility to be a Gospel proclaimer by simply living a good life in front of other people. It is often quoted and attributed to Saint Francis of Assisi of saying "Share the Gospel at all times, and when needed, use words." While our lifestyle and behaviors do serve as the platform for people to hear what we have to say, we are ultimately responsible to verbally express the Gospel through words.

The Example

Let me give you an example as to why our good behavior will never be good enough for people to see and believe. There is a story that Dr. Al Mohler tells of a preacher preaching in a rather large church. During the musical part of worship in one of the services an older man has a heart attack. Since it was a big church there were several physicians in the congregation who attended to the man rather quickly. They immediately called the paramedics and moved the man out of the worship center. The pastor got up to preach, and as he did, one of the physicians came back into the worship center and gave a hand signal of crossing his hands and moving them back out (much like the beginning of a baseball umpire's safe signal) to the pastor and to the unintended choir who was sitting behind the pastor. The pastor interpreted the sign, thought everything was okay, and did not abbreviate the message but preached it all. After the service, the pastor eventually made his way to the car where his wife was waiting, and he could tell she was very angry. As he got into the car, his wife told him he was the most egotistical and insensitive man she knew because he did not stop the service but preached a full sermon when a guy had died. She had also seen the signal the physician gave to the pastor while she was sitting in the choir. She interpreted the signal to mean the man had died. The pastor responded, "What do you mean? The physician came in and said everything was okay." The pastor's wife retorted, "No he did not. He told you the man was dead." The pastor quickly got out of his car, and ran inside to find the physician and asked him what he meant by his signal. The physician replied "that the man was fine and safe." The pastor looked at him both relieved and bothered and said, "Next time give me a clearer sign."

A Christian's good life of Gospel living may be sending all the right signals in the mind of the believer, but those signals are being sent from the perspective of an individual with a biblical worldview. I believe that it would be safe to say that a nonbeliever does not possess a biblical worldview, and, therefore, they will very likely misinterpret those signals as something entirely different. They may see the good works of someone who is helping out those in need as an effort to usher in a utopia of sorts in our current world, or they may see the same signals as someone who is seeking to develop some good Karma for themselves in an effort to reach Nirvana. No one will receive the Gospel message without hearing it clearly communicated with words.

Scriptural Understanding

There are passages of Scripture such as 1 Peter 2:12 that say, "*Keep your conduct among the Gentiles honorable, so that when they speak against you as evildoers, they may see your good deeds and glorify God on the day of visitation.*" Such a passage may seem to support a notion of people turning to give glory to God because of the good behavior of Christians. The idea comes from the very teaching of Jesus in Matthew 5:16 that says, "*let your light shine before others, so that they may see your good works and give glory to your Father who is in heaven.*" But as is always the case, students of the Word must keep the entirety of Scripture in mind when arriving at the truth in which we are to live. For if we turn to Romans 10, Paul expresses his heart's desire for the nation of Israel to be saved. Paul speaks of how they have been misguided as to how to obtain righteousness and believe that righteousness is gained by the keeping of the Law. On the contrary, Paul explains that righteousness is secured by faith in Jesus Christ and is available for "*all who call on him.*" (Rom. 10:12) This leads Paul to ask a series of rhetorical questions and arrive at the answer in verses 14-17,

"How then will they call on him in whom they have not believed? And how are they to believe in him of whom they have

never HEARD? And how are they to HEAR without someone preaching? And how are they to preach unless they are sent? As it is written, 'How beautiful are the feet of those who preach the good news!' But they have not all obeyed the gospel. For Isaiah says, 'Lord, who has believed what he has HEARD from us?' So, faith comes from HEARING, and HEARING (emphasis mine) *through the word of Christ."*

People will only ever come to Christ after they have HEARD the message of Christ or the Gospel. They will never respond to the Gospel by just seeing God's people be kind or do good works.

With the explanation of the Gospel well understood and the warning that by our Gospel living we will never lead anyone to salvation without words, we can now move on and understand why and how our lives should be characterized by the Gospel message itself.

Gospel Living

Chapter 2:

Gospel Lifestyle—Love and Justice

"It is more accurate to say that we are saved by believing the gospel, and then we are transformed in every part of our minds, hearts, and lives by believing the gospel more and more deeply as life goes on."[9]- Timothy Keller

As a parent, there is constant tension day-to-day between loving your child and at the same time being just in punishing them. The child sees the punishment as harsh and

---

[9] Timothy Keller, "Center Church: Doing Balanced Gospel-Centered Ministry in Your City," (Grand Rapids, MI: Zondervan, 2012), 48.

unfair treatment that lacks any resemblance of love. I mean how many times do you hear of a child thanking their parent for loving them in the moment of punishment? The reason is that a child or person being punished hardly ever feels like the punishment is fair. If you are an objective observer of a punishable offense, you could more accurately issue the just penalty for the crime, but the one issuing the punishment and receiving the punishment are often subjective in their view of justice. The child being punished does not think their offense is too bad, so they feel their just punishment should be a wagging finger followed by the statement, "Never do that again." On the other hand, the parent is greatly grieved by what has just happened and has a desire to issue a punishment that will be so unpleasant that the child will never again conceive of doing what they did. In the end, both parties often feel unsatisfied with what was intended to be a just penalty because as sinful human beings we have a misguided idea of what is true justice.

    As an adult, I view my punishments as a child differently. I remember what seemed to be terrifying punishments in the past as a kid and view them through the lens of a loving parent that wants to teach and protect my children. I see the love that was shown to me by my parents even though it did not feel much like love at the time. As a parent, I know that my children do not comprehend the consequences of some of the things they do, so I give them a set of rules and expectations. When they choose to willfully disobey those rules, with love I issue a (hopefully) just punishment to deter them from breaking those rules again. We all probably have a specific instance in our life where we received a punishment we did not like but look back and treasure the love our authority figures showed us and principles they taught us.

With this kind of tension, it is clear why we have such a hard time understanding the beautiful blend of God's love and justice. We possess concepts of love, due to our limited abilities, that cannot marry the ideas of God's love and justice at the same time. We develop teachings about God that are birthed out of our human experiences and reasoning that say, "God is love and there is no way He would let anyone go to hell." After all, we tend to believe that if we love someone, we will overlook their glaring flaws as if they are not there even though those flaws are destructive to others, themselves, and even ourselves. This kind of thinking is more of a study of "anthropology" instead of "theology." The genesis of those thoughts finds their origin in humanity and are absent from God's spoken Word to us, the Bible. We must understand these two most essential aspects of the Gospel message so that we rightly understand God and correctly apply the Gospel to life until it becomes a lifestyle.

Before we go on, it is important to note that God is One and not divided. So, when God executes justice on someone, He is not battling within Himself with the aspect of love, mercy, grace, and forgiveness. His attributes are never at war against each other.

Love and Justice: Can't Have One Without the Other

Unlike the rest of the attributes and aspects of the Gospel that we will encounter in this book, we are not going to define love and justice separately but define them together as love is not without justice and justice is not without love. Love is defined by William Farley in his book *Outrageous Mercy*, which defines God's love as "an intense, all powerful, merciful desire for the eternal happiness of creatures who are at war with Him and who intentionally rebel against Him and they deserve death."[10] Notice the definition contains an intense caring that we could never know in our own experience because the intensity of love for someone who does not love us back often wanes when love is not reciprocated. This is a love that is unfathomable in our human experience.

---

[10] William P. Farley, "Outrageous Mercy: Rediscover the Radical Nature of Christianity," (Grand Rapids, MI: Baker Books, 2004), 44.

Jonathan Kyle

The love of God is extravagant upon all of His creation. There is no lie spoken when you say to an unsaved person "God loves you!" Generally speaking, God shows His love to every human being by giving them life. He then sustains those who live in rebellion against Him by providing for their basic needs (Matt. 5:45). God blesses every human being with good things (James 1:17). The greatest act of love that God has shown to all of humanity is that while we wanted nothing to do with Him, He provided a way for us to receive forgiveness and be in a right relationship with Him again (Rom. 5:8, John 15:13).

However, the love of God is lavished even greater upon those He calls His children. "Wait!" some of you might say "Are not all people God's children?" The answer is "No." John answers that question for us in john 1:12 when he says, *"But to all who did receive him, who believed in his name, he gave the right to BECOME CHILDREN OF GOD* (emphasis mine)." (Let me supply you with a short list of how God's love is specific for His children:

- His love for you is eternal and never failing (Psalm 103:17, 136:1).
- His love for you is inseparable and never leaves you alone (Romans 8:38-39, Deut. 31:6).

Gospel Living

- His love for you is working all things out for your good and, most of all, for His glory (Romans 8:28).
- His love for you is a refuge and safe place in time of trouble (Psalm 36:7).
- His love for you is mighty to save you from your sin (Zephaniah 3:17).
- His love for you is giving you an eternal inheritance (1 Peter 1:4-5)
- His love for you is a guide that restores your soul (Psalm 23).

And this list could go on and on with His abundant love for those whom He has saved. But I want to direct our attention back to the necessity of seeing God's love connected with His justice. I fear this connection is neglected when we ponder the love of God in the Gospel message. This connection will be helpful as we consider how we should live with love and justice in our own lives.

John Piper explains the necessity of the blend of God's love and justice by saying, "If God were not just, there would be no demand for his Son to suffer and die. And if God were not loving, there would be no willingness for his Son to suffer and die. But God is both just and loving. Therefore, his love is willing to meet the demands of his justice."[11] Piper's explanation gives us good understanding as to why the cross of Christ was necessary and at the same time why Jesus even goes through with this most grueling of all punishments. The reason is because God is love, and the definition of his love is inseparable from His justice.

For those who do not understand the connection of God's love and justice, it is difficult to grasp why God, who is love, would ever send anyone to hell. Mark Driscoll illustrates this point well when he responds to people who say God is mean when He allow people to go to Hell. He says, "Jesus suffered and died for mean people. A God who will suffer and die for mean people is not mean," asserts Driscoll. "In fact, such a God alone is altogether loving; to be condemned by a God of perfect love shows how damnable our sin truly is."[12] Driscoll flips that whole argument on its head by pointing out what we discovered earlier. We are sinners living in direct and willful disobedience to God who deserve the just punishment of eternal separation from God in Hell. God cannot overlook what seem to be insignificant little trespasses of sin. This thought harkens back to the opening illustration. The guilty child feels that justice

---

[11] John Piper, "Fifty Reason Why Jesus Came to Die," (Wheaton, IL: Crossway, 2006), 20.
[12] Mark Driscoll, "6 Questions About Hell Pt. 2," *ChurchLeaders*, (March 23, 2016), http://www.churchleaders.com/pastors/pastor-articles/149648-149648-mark-driscoll-to-hell-with-hell_part2-html.html.

is simply a threat to "never do what you did again." I believe this kind of thinking carries with it the idea that God is OBLIGATED to forgive my sins because of His love. The reality is that God is NOT OBLIGATED in any way to just overlook our sins. His justice will not permit it!

God cannot just sweep our sins under the rug of the universe because He has a holy wrath built up against those sins.[13] Once again, the problem with this thought of God being mean for sending people to Hell stems from our human idea of love being merely simple affection. When we think of God's love as merely affection, then we resolve to think the goodness of God will overlook our sin because of His affection for us. Our idea of affection causes us to misinterpret passages of Scripture such as 1 John 4:8 that says, *"Anyone who does not love does not know God, because God is love."* We read this passage and immediately think of God embracing us and the safety and security that comes from being loved by God. This is a comfort that we should receive when we read passages of Scripture that speak of God's love for us, but this is not the complete picture of God's love. The more complete nature of God's love is found in His demonstration of love found in the very next verse that says, *"In this the love of God was*

---

[13] John Piper, "Fifty Reasons Why Jesus Came to Die," (Wheaton, IL: Crossway, 2006), 21.

made manifest among us, that God sent his only Son into the world, so that we might live through him." The complete picture of God's love is that He intensely loves us giving us happiness that is found only in Him but His love requires there to be justice. So, in verse 9 we see that God's love sent Jesus to the cross so that all who believe by faith may be justified and fully embrace the completeness that comes in having a right relationship with God.

That is what I cherish so much about the love of God. We do not know God's love just because He tells us with His words, even though His word alone would be good enough, but we know His love because He showed it with His actions. Think about this truth for a second. It is one thing for me to tell my wife that I love her. But my wife believes those words not just because I said them but because of the 10 years of faithfulness to her, the unending service to her, countless bouquets of flowers and gifts, and sacrifices that I have made for her. Love demonstrates itself in action. The Apostle John says this in 1 John 3:16, *"By this we know love, that he laid down his life for us…"* Christian, we know what great sacrificial love is because Jesus laid down His life as a sacrifice on our behalf.

But do we really understand what a great sacrifice Jesus made for us? I fear in our cross-saturated culture that we let the words "Jesus died on the cross for the sins of the world" slide off of our tongues without

Gospel Living

much understanding of the sacrifice. I know that I am guilty of this. I once heard a story by Ed Stetzer as he preached a message at The Summit Church in North Carolina that gives us a glimpse of the tremendous sacrifice Jesus made. Ed tells a story of when he was a boy. His family had come upon some hard times and moved to Florida with his grandparents because his grandparents owned an apartment building that they could rent for cheap. Ed shares how it was not the greatest of places and they often had problems with their toilets backing up. One day when the sewage backed up, his grandpa showed up and tossed him a shovel and told him to go digging with him in the backyard. The invitation to dig up the backyard was very appealing to Ed as a young boy. Every boy wants to dig in their backyard for dinosaur bones and treasure. After several minutes of digging, they struck something hard that had a lid on it. Ed was from the city and knew nothing about septic tanks, so he was excited to see what was under the lid. However, when the lid popped open, Ed's excitement quickly turned to disgust as his grandpa charged him with the task of trying to discover what was clogging up the tank. During the task of unclogging the tank the unthinkable happened. Ed fell knee deep into the septic tank.[14]

---

[14] Ed Stetzer, "Representing Jesus and His Kingdom: 2 Corinthians 5:16-21", *The Summit Church*. Podcast audio, August 9, 2015.

Jonathan Kyle

As you choke back down what you most recently ate, think about the visceral response that you just received when you imagined Ed knee deep in human excrement. Then imagine Jesus in all His glory sitting in the throne room of Heaven submitting Himself to the will of the Father by taking on the flesh of humanity. God, Himself, walked around in the muck and the mire of our sin-filled world. And instead of being disgusted by the dirtiness of sin, the Bible says that "When *he saw the crowds, he had compassion for them, because they were harassed and helpless, like sheep without a shepherd*" (Matt. 9:36). Jesus' mission was not to ridicule humanity for their unlimited sin, but to make a way to reconcile us all to God through the cross.

Do you see that the motivation of such a great act of love flows from God's necessity for justice? The easy thing for God to have done would have been to keep Jesus in heaven and affectionately love His creation by forgetting about their sin and permitting them all to join in Heaven. But obviously, this is not what has happened. Why? Because God is both love and justice. He cannot leave sin unpunished. If He were to do so, He would cease being God. John Stott explains this when he says, "If God does not justly punish sin, he would be 'unjust to himself'... he would destroy both himself and us."[15]

God's justice will not permit wrong to be unpunished. So, when people believe that God is good and therefore, will forgive sin, they really have a problem that their god is not good enough. William Farley says to this point, "How could any being that does not hate evil with an absolute hatred be good? A God that does not abhor evil and express wrath toward it would not be the holy, pure, and perfect God portrayed in the Bible."[16]

There are two reasons why we as humans typically have a problem with the idea of the wrath of God which is executed through His justice for sins. First, the experience that we have in our context is that of wrath being evil. We observe someone being threatened or being done wrong who blows up in violent anger taking vengeance on whoever opposes them. But this wrathful person always has an idea of justice that goes beyond what true justice should be. Here is an example. I used to love playing pranks on people as a young teenager. But it did not take me long to figure out that the person I pranked would, in return, prank me back in a way that was more devious, at least in my mind. This would result in me getting back at them in a way that was escalated in the amount of torture inflicted. Each of us

---
[15] William P. Farley, "Outrageous Mercy: Rediscover the Radical Nature of Christianity," (Grand Rapids, MI: Baker Books, 2004), 41.
[16] Ibid., 42.

was seeking justice for our wrong, but our justice was always skewed and never perfect. We must remember that God's wrath is a response of perfect goodness to wickedness and evil. God's wrath and justice is always equal to what is deserved. As humans we are not able to imitate such justice and wrath.

Second, we have a pride issue that causes us to see that our offense is not so bad; therefore, we believe our offense does not deserve the drastic consequences of Hell. That is why many people believe they are going to Heaven even though they have not received Christ. Their pride leads them to believe they are a good person.[17]

So where in the Scriptures do we find this example of love and justice?

The Cross-The Example of Love and Justice

There is no clearer picture in Scripture to see where love and justice meet than Jesus on the cross. We have been talking about it this whole chapter, so this should come as no surprise. We arrive at the cross to see what Jesus said there and how people responded to His death, so that you can see that love and justice met together at Calvary.

---

[17] Ibid., 43.

Gospel Living

Let's take a look at the account that Mark gives us of Jesus' dying breath on the cross in Mark 15:33-39,

"And when the sixth hour had come, there was darkness over the whole land until the night hour. And at the ninth hour Jesus cried with a loud voice, 'Eloi, Eloi, lema sabachthani?' which means, 'My God, my God, why have you forsaken me?' And some of the bystanders hearing it said, 'Behold, he is calling Elijah.' And someone ran and filled a sponge with sour wine, put it on a reed and gave it to him to drink, saying, 'Wait, let us see whether Elijah will come to take him down.' And Jesus uttered a loud cry and breathed his last. And the curtain of the temple was torn in to, from top to bottom. And when the centurion, who stood facing him, saw that in this way he breathed his last, he said, 'Truly this man was the Son of God!'"

The love of Jesus is clearly communicated when He allowed Himself to be taken captive even though He was guilty of no crime. His love for His enemies SCREAMS with every lash that ripped open His back. And His love PENETRATES every dark and deceptive heart when the nails were driven through His feet and hands. Truly, "*Greater love has no one than this, that someone lay down his life for his friends*" (John 15:13). But Jesus not only laid His life down for His friends but also His enemies as Romans 5:8 says, "*but God shows his love for us in that while we were still sinners, Christ died for us."*

This love of Jesus was so evident on the cross that even a master killer recognized His abundant love. Mark gives us insight into the centurion's response to Jesus' death. This centurion who had seen hundreds of men die the very same death marveled at the way in which Jesus died, so that Mark leads us to realize that the centurion's basic understanding was that Jesus was *"Truly...the Son of God."*

The wrath of God that was being executed on the sins of the world is clearly understood by Jesus' question on the cross *"Why have you forsaken me?"* The only clear-cut explanation of the abandonment of God the Father from His Son is the Father turning away from Jesus because of the sin that has been placed upon Him as the divine substitute for mankind. In these words of Jesus, we see and understand the justice that has taken place as Jesus paid the price for the sins of man through abandonment from God and death. The awesome thing about Jesus' words on the cross is that they are a direct quotation of Psalm 22:1. That Psalm goes on to speak of the anticipated salvation that the Lord will bring. So, while the price of sin is paid for through His death, Jesus conquers those penalties of sin by rising from the grave three days later.

The Apostle Peter sums up Jesus' selfless love and justice well in 1 Peter 2:24

that says, *"He himself bore our sins in his body on the tree, that we might die to sin and live to righteousness. By his wounds you have been healed."*

Applying Love and Justice to Life Until it Becomes a Lifestyle

Jesus told His disciples on the night that He was betrayed, *"By this all people will know that you are my disciples, if you have love for one another."* (John 13:35) Jesus did not say that people will know that you are my followers by what you wear or do not wear, what music you listen to or do not listen to, the movies that you watch or do not watch, but rather you will be known by your love for one another. The focal point of the Gospel is love, therefore, the evident characteristic of someone who has been transformed by the Gospel message is LOVE.

Is that what you observe in your community of believers? Is love clearly evident by everyone who enters the doors of your gathering space? Or think about this question: is love clearly seen by those who are around Christians in their workplace, school, or home? The sad reality is that most Christians are not known for what they do but rather what they do not do. We are quick to point out our stance against a certain politician or the latest social issue, but how quick are we to show love to those on the opposite side of the spectrum from us or seek to meet the justice issue of the poor in our community? I am not promoting the idea of love that just accepts everyone's position as valid for the sake of just getting along. What I am suggesting is that just because someone believes something different than you does not make them an enemy nor does it prevent you from caring about their needs and championing their success. This does not mean that you agree with them but that does not stop you from loving them. In fact, that person is never going to be even remotely interested in the Gospel message until they see the love of God manifested in you as you love them for who they are. Then you will have earned yourself the platform on which to speak the Gospel, and they will be willing to hear it because your love has broken down their barriers.

The elementary practice of love should begin within our own local body of believers. Is your church known by the lost for their love for one another or on how they cannot get along? If you have a perception problem as a church in your community, that perception did not arise out of nowhere. To live a life that is transformed by the Gospel of love in community begins with learning how to love those people within your community. First, we must commit to praying for one another within our churches. God does something amazing within our hearts when we start carrying to God in prayer the burdens of someone else as if they are our own and asking Him to intervene in their lives. All of a sudden, we start caring about the outcome of their job interview, sickness, daily time with God, or mission trip. When we are praying for other people, we actually celebrate and give God the glory together for the answered prayer. We learn how to mourn with them in their times of trial. I challenge you to begin praying through your small group roll, church directory, or get involved with a prayer chain at your church.

Second, embrace humility by considering others as being more important than yourself by looking out for their interests above your own (Phil. 2:3-4). See yourself as a servant to your brothers and sisters in Christ and look for even small ways in which you can serve them. Put yourself in servant roles in church where the majority of people do not even know what you do but are recipients of your serving acts of love on a week-to-week basis. Intentionally sacrifice some of your free time to serve a widow, orphan, handicapped, elderly person, or someone in need that is inside your faith family.

Next, share with others when they have need (Acts 2:42-47). The obvious sharing is that of money and resources. That means you need to be aware of needs around you by listening intently to the conversations that you have with others. Also, do not be afraid to ask the staff of the church where they might know of a need.

Needs abound, the hardest thing is being made aware of the needs and partnering those needs with people who can meet them. Some of you have already dismissed this portion of loving others within your congregation because you are barely getting by financially. I would encourage you to seek ways within your finances to give to others. This may mean seeking help from a financial counselor to help you plan an effective budget so that you can consistently give out of what God has already given to you. In addition, there are other ways to love and serve others that are not financial in nature. There are some people within your congregation who need a listening ear. Others have need for community. Still other struggling parents have need of getting out of the house to spend some time alone. Keep your eyes open and be vigilant for an opportunity where you can step in and show your love to them by sharing what you have to meet their need.

    Other ways of showing love may look like walking through a tough time with someone. One that is often overlooked in showing love to others is holding each other accountable in the faith. Like a child that we discipline out of love to keep them from a destructive behavior, we need to hold each other accountable in love to keep someone from shipwrecking their faith.

    All of these aspects of love in the community of faith should be aspects of love in our personal lives as well. We should practice them within our own families and amongst our friends and neighborhoods. These must be intentional acts of love. Being known as a person full of God's love will not be given to you by accident. Pray and ask God to give you practical and creative ideas to show the love of Christ to people around you.

Love that is motivated by the Gospel should not just be shown to the brothers and sisters in the faith. This amazing love that was demonstrated to us while we were still enemies of God should be shown to those who are still opposed to the will of God. Just as Christ had compassion on the multitudes in Matthew 9:36, we too should have compassion on the lost people that are around us. We must see through what they are wearing, saying, or doing and understand that they are like "sheep without a shepherd." They are lost out on their own and headed for certain destruction if we do not act in love towards them by sharing the truth of the Gospel with them through our words. Maybe before we share the life changing power of the Gospel with our words, they must see the effects of that Gospel message in our lives shown in how we love them. We might even need to ask ourselves if we really love them enough to serve and walk alongside them for months or even years before they surrender their will to God and believe by faith that He is their

Savior. The love of Christ, demonstrated on the cross, should compel us to show that same sacrificial love to others so they might know how they can be saved.

Justice! We must stand up against any injustice that we are made aware of around us. If that is standing up against bullies at school or fighting for basic services for the poor in your city, we cannot sit idly by allowing injustice to take place. So go and volunteer at the local organizations in your city that protect the rights of the poor. If God gives you a vision for how you can meet the needs of the poor, then begin by simply being obedient with what you have and who you can help around you. My brother, Jamie and his wife Kelli did this very thing. After many years of assisting the poor on a personal level by helping people find jobs, transporting them to places of work, and financially assisting with food, they partnered together with Kelli's dad, Terry Johns to start The Refuge. The Refuge is a nonprofit organization that seeks to combine the resources that are offered in the community to help people to move from need to sustainability. In talking with them, they have a real passion to avoid giving people handouts but instead, give them the tools necessary to reach sustainability while maintaining their dignity. They have now grown into one of the more respectable resource centers for those in need in our hometown. God does some amazing things through the simple obedience of His people.

There are a lot of great organizations out there who are letting their desire for justice motivate their love for people who have been taken advantage of. One of the clearest examples of this blend of love and justice is found in the organizations that have dedicated themselves to ending modern day slavery. One of those organizations is the International Justice Mission. There are some 21 million people in the world who are kept in some modern form of slavery. IJM makes it their mission that these 21 million who do not have a voice have a representative who is fighting for their God-given value. They make it clear that their mission is inspired by God's call to love all people and seek justice.[18] I encourage you to go to their website (ijm.org) and read the countless stories of where IJM has worked together with local authorities to free people from forced labor, improper property seizure, sex trafficking, and citizen's rights abuse.

There are other ways to stand up against injustice like giving financially to organizations like IJM or by serving with these organizations. Your main responsibility is to be aware of injustice and do your part to make sure justice is attained.

---

[18] "Who We Are," International Justice Mission, April 10, 2016, https://www.ijm.org/our-work.

In the end, the greatest way to attract the lost and change the perception of your faith family is by standing up against injustice and serving your community out of love.

Living Out the Gospel Questions
1. Do you still see conflict between God's love and justice? Why or why not?
2. How are you currently living out love and justice in your community?
3. What are some other ways that you can show love and live out justice?
4. What has stood out to you that you learned or never thought of before about love and justice?
5. How can you promote love and justice within your own church?

Gospel Living

Chapter 3:

Gospel Lifestyle—Grace

"The gospel is not only the most important message in all of history; it is the only essential message in all of history. Yet we allow thousands of professing Christians to live their entire lives without clearly understanding it and experiencing the joy of living by it."[19] Jerry Bridges

Through this book on Gospel living, I want you to understand that Christians should not behave a certain way because we can change the world, because it is what our

---

[19] Jerry Bridges, "The Discipline of Grace," (Colorado Springs, CO: NavPres, 1994), 46.

parents taught us, or because we go to church. We behave differently because of the Gospel. It is because of Christ's sacrifice that we live differently. While those above reasons may be fine, if the Gospel does not serve as our root motivation, then we are just going through the motions and our behavior will change when the above reasons change. That is not living according to God's Word.

Before we carry on much further, one thing we must notice is that these aspects of the Gospel are all attributes of God. And attributes do not describe God, but God describes the attribute. For example, we do not say "God is love" and seek to gather our understanding of who God is based on our own earthly definition of love. Instead, "God is love" helps Christians understand what love is because of who they know God to be in how He showed love and what He says about love. God describes love; love does not describe God. "*By this we know love, that he laid down his life for us…*" *(*1 John 3:16a). The second thing we need to understand is that God is innately love just as much as He is innately justice or holiness. Therefore, when we see Scripture say "God shows more grace" or "God abounds in grace," it means that His grace abounds more on us because we are sinners and not that He possesses more of it than other aspects.

Jonathan Kyle

Undeserved Favor

Grace is a word that we throw around a lot but may not understand. At the same time grace is something that we experience daily yet we are not always aware. Our unfamiliarity with grace is comically communicated by a scene in my favorite Christmas movie of all time, *National Lampoons Christmas Vacation*. Clark Griswold (Chevy Chase) is leading his entire family at the dinner table and calls upon his hard of hearing and senile Aunt Bethany to say "Grace" since it is her 80th Christmas. Aunt Bethany is unsure of what has been said until someone shouts at her "GRACE!" Bethany then responds, "Grace...she died 30 years ago." After some clarification from her equally senile husband, Bethany bows her head and proceeds to lead the entire family in...The Pledge of Allegiance. Now, we might be able to quickly realize that the grace we are talking about is not a woman's name nor is it the prayer of blessing over a meal (OR THE PLEDGE OF ALLEGIANCE), but what exactly is grace?

Grace is simply defined as undeserved favors. That means God deals with believers not based on what we deserve but based on our need. He shows His goodness and generosity on all who believe even when as sinners they deserve death. Grace is essentially rewarding individuals who deserve punishment. The Bible says in

Romans 6:23, *"For the wages of sin is death..."* I established previously that everyone who has ever walked this earth is a sinner. That means that everyone, as a payment for their sins, deserves death. But Paul continues on in the same verse and says, *"but the free gift of God is eternal life in Christ Jesus our Lord."* So, everyone who believes in Jesus Christ as their Savior and repents of their sins receives the deserved gift of Christ upon themselves albeit undeserved by them.

When someone fully understands this transaction of undeserved favor by God to them in salvation, then they will be able to grasp the fact that there is nothing they can physically do to gain salvation from God. That understanding is the very reason John Newton penned the words of the most famous hymn of all time, "Amazing Grace." Newton was amazed by God's grace because he knew that prior to becoming a Christian, the actions of his life fully deserved the punishment of God. Newton did not become a Christian until his late twenties. Up until then he had been a slave trader in West Africa and was a godless man. For example, he had a black slave as his mistress. When he caught her in a sexual relationship with a black man, he beat the man to death with his shovel. The man he beat to death was actually his mistress' real husband. Moreover, on the long voyages across the Atlantic, he and his mates would rape some of the women being transported to their North American masters. Though many of them would arrive pregnant with his seed, he was hard and indifferent to the fate of these women and their children. So, after his conversion, Newton looked at the cross with amazement. There he saw grace—Christ suffering in agony of God's wrath in HIS place, so that God could reward HIM with eternal life. The grace that God showed Newton (and everyone else on the earth) stunned him, and as a result it changed his life forever.[20]

As followers of Christ reading this book, our sins may be different than Newton's, but God's grace works the same way for us and our countless sins. Grace appears most perfectly in the knowledge of our sin revealed at the cross. Only Gospel-centered Christians find grace amazing. I have a personal practice I do that helps me keep God's free gift of grace in perspective. Occasionally, I will reflect back on my life to the moments of great failure and seasons of open rebellion in my Christian walk. While the temptation can be to let guilt overwhelm me and beat myself up over past sins, I use it to remind myself that God has forgiven me and saved me DESPITE my moments and seasons of failure. This truth gives me confidence that if Christ receives me and

---

[20] William P. Farley, "Outrageous Mercy: Rediscover the Radical Nature of Christianity," (Grand Rapids, MI: Baker Books, 2004), 52.

gives me salvation based on nothing that I do, then there is nothing I can do to unearn what I did not earn in the first place. I am His and forgiven by His willful free gift of grace.

The Promise of a New Heart

The cross is at the center of the Gospel and could be the biblical example for each one of these characteristics of the Gospel, but let's look at some examples throughout the Scriptures. For the example of grace, we will go to the Old Testament and look at a passage of Scripture in Ezekiel 36. Ezekiel is a prophet called by God to warn the nation of Israel to turn back toward God or face the coming destruction of Jerusalem. After the fall of Jerusalem in 586BC, the message that God gives Ezekiel is a message of hope and restoration. Near the passage that we are going to look at is the New Covenantal promises that God will "*give you a new heart, and a new spirit [God] will put within you*" (vs. 26a). No longer will God's presence be at a physical location for the nation of Israel, but He will be inside of all who believe in Christ. The fulfillment of this promise takes place at the Day of Pentecost in Acts 2. This gift of the Spirit is truly something that no one can deserve, but hear the message that God wants Ezekiel to tell His people before He promises this gift. In Ezekiel 36:22, God says to Ezekiel, "*Therefore say to the house of Israel, Thus says the Lord God; It is not for your sake, O house of Israel, that I am about to act, but for the sake of my holy name, which you have profaned among the nations to which you came."* God makes it abundantly clear that what He is going to do through the nation of Israel is not based on their obedience to Him. Instead, God tells us that DESPITE all of their disobedience He is going to use them to make HIS name known throughout all of the nations.

There are two things that we can see from this passage about the grace of God and why He freely lavishes it upon His people. The first reason alluded to above in defining grace is that His amazing grace causes us to be extremely grateful because we know the magnitude of our own depravity. Following the promises in verse 26 of a "new heart" and the "Spirit" in verses 29-30, God says He will deliver them from their unrighteousness and abundantly bless them in all the land. In verse 31, He tells them the effect of this blessing when He says, *"Then you will remember your evil ways, and your deeds that were not good, and you will loathe yourselves for your iniquities and your abominations."* God is saying after I bless you and your land you will begin to wonder why I am doing this for you. After you look back on the past and realize you did nothing to deserve it, you will see the wretchedness of your sin and understand the grace of God.

Gospel Living

The second and the most important reason God pours out His grace so freely is for His glory. Verse 32 says this "*It is not for your sake that I will act, declares the Lord God; let that be known to you…*" The nation of Israel is going to be the recipient of this tremendous blessing of cleanliness and abundance in crops, but the blessing is not to be used for themselves but for the glory of God in the entire world. In other words, the nation of Israel is the blessed and the blessers. Christian, you and I as recipients of God's AMAZING GRACE are greatly blessed by this free gift of salvation from our sins but we are to be the conduits of grace to the world around us so they too may be blessed. I will talk more about that in the application section.

While this example is a clear picture of the grace of God on the people of Israel, all throughout the Old Testament God in His grace is choosing people like Noah, Abraham, Joseph, Moses, David, etc. None of these heroes in the faith did anything to warrant the favor of God in their lives, but God lavishly poured out His grace upon them and blessed both them and the people around them through them.

$47.50

Undoubtedly, there are many stories of undeserved favors that take place on a daily basis throughout the world. In fact, just

Jonathan Kyle

yesterday I returned home with my family from a two-day getaway in the mountains to the surprise of a home makeover that took place while we were gone. People from our church, the private school at our church, and our extended family had worked feverishly tearing out our floors and laying down hardwood throughout the whole house. They cleaned out our entire garage, built shelves and then organized and labeled all our belongings in the garage. They painted the porch, rehung shutters, pressure washed the house and driveway, landscaped the yard, put tile down in the bathroom, and organized all of our closets in less than 2 full days. Our friends and neighbors said it looked like an extreme makeover TV show without the cameras. My wife and I were so surprised! I still get emotional when I think of the extreme kindness and generosity that was shown to me and my family. While the people who performed this amazing act of kindness would say that my family and I deserved this, I still believe the makeover was an undeserved grace gift.

Many of the people who served my family went unnamed and wanted no credit for anything that they did. However, my family and I want to tell the world of this great gift of grace so we have made our gratitude known on social media, written "Thank You" letters, and continuously invite our friends and family over so they can see what has been done. And as time moves on and the

Gospel Living

newness of the upgrades of our house wear off, I will never forget this unbelievable act of grace that was shown because it was so undeserved and so impactful in my life.

There is another story of modern grace that has been told for years now about the former mayor of New York City, Fiorello La Guardia. The direct account of the story I am about to share with you is not proven or documented in history, but the regular actions of La Guardia make the story impossible to refute as well. Whatever the case, whether fiction or nonfiction, the point of this account speaks of the undeserved favors that God has shown to believers.

"We can start this story in the winter of 1935. The nation was in the throes of the great depression. It is hard for us to imagine in today's affluent society just how desperate those days were. There were long lines of hungry people standing in front of soup kitchens waiting for something to eat. Jobs were virtually nonexistent, and money was as precious as it was scarce. There was a man by the name of Fiorello La Guardia who was the mayor of New York City during those dark days. LaGuardia seemed to have a genuine heartfelt love for the common man, especially the downtrodden. One time, during a newspaper strike, he spent his Sunday mornings reading the funny papers over the radio, and with all the appropriate inflections. Why? He did not want the children of New York to be deprived of that

Jonathan Kyle

little bit of enjoyment. He was well- known for his blustery outbursts against the bums that exploited the poor. He was completely unpredictable and full of surprises. One night he showed up at a night court in one of the poorest wards of the city; and that is where this phase of our story begins. He dismissed the presiding judge for the evening and sent him home to his family. Then the mayor himself took over the bench. As it happened on that bitterly cold night, a tattered old woman stood before the bench, she was accused of stealing a loaf of bread. With quivering lips and tear-filled eyes, she admitted to the theft. But, she added, my daughter's husband has deserted her, she is sick, and her children are crying because they have nothing to eat. The shopkeeper, however, refused to drop the charges. 'It's a bad neighborhood, Your Honor, she's guilty,' he shouted. 'The law must be upheld; she's got to be punished to teach other people a lesson.' LaGuardia knew that her accuser was right. The very office that he swore to uphold required that he enforce the letter of the law. LaGuardia sighed. He turned to the old women and said 'I've got to punish you; the law makes no exceptions.' He then pronounced the sentence. The old woman shuddered when she heard the words, ten dollars or ten days in jail. But already the judge was reaching into his pocket. He pulled out a ten-dollar bill and threw it into his hat. 'Here's the ten-dollar fine, which I now remit. Furthermore, I'm fining everyone in this courtroom fifty cents for living in a town where a person has to steal bread so that her grandchildren can eat. Mr. Bailiff, collect the fines and give them to the defendant.' Sitting in that courtroom that night were about seventy petty criminals, a few New York policemen, and her accuser, a fuming, red-faced, storekeeper. The bewildered old grandmother left the courtroom with $47.50. This was enough to buy groceries for several months."[21]

True or not, this story depicts what God in His love and justice must do in punishing sinners, and how God in His abundant grace makes a way for sinners to be in right standing with Him through paying the debt Himself. I challenge you to stop and give thanks to God for His amazing grace shown to you.

Applying Grace to Life Until It Becomes a Lifestyle

As individuals who have been shown abundant grace, our lives should be marked by amazing grace. In fact, Paul's letter to Titus makes this clear when he says, *"For the GRACE of God has appeared, bringing salvation for all people, training us to renounce ungodliness and worldly passions,*

---

[21] Delmar L. Legar, "A Story of Grace" (Feast of Tabernacles, Grand Junction, Colorado, 2002)

and to live self-controlled, upright, and godly lives in the present...zealous for good works." (2:11-12, 14) Grace is never deserved but the thankful response from the recipient to the giver is always deserved. I want to make myself clear before going any further; God does not give us grace so that He will have followers. Remember, God does not need us but rather we need Him. God is not so desperate for a relationship with humanity that He in some sense "buys" our affection. That is not the case at all. Instead, God loves His creation so much that He does the right thing by extending grace to helpless sinners.

Paul then makes the connection for Titus and the church that the appropriate response to an "undeserved favor" of God is to live lives in submission and obedience to the will of God. We apply grace to life until it becomes a lifestyle by turning from sin, living with self-control, walking in purity, emulating the example of Christ in character, and desiring to do good, grace-filled works for others. Essentially, our good works and character do not gain our salvation but prove that we are grateful recipients of the grace of God in salvation.

Continuing my thought from the Ezekiel 36 passage, our appropriate response to the grace of God is to share this free gift of salvation with the world. The often-quoted statement about evangelism explains this: "Evangelism is just one beggar telling another beggar where to find bread." If you have received something that is free and fulfilling, then the most loving thing to do is share that blessing with others. But there is a bigger reason why we should share the Gospel with others and that is so that the glory of God would be spread throughout the earth. Our existence on earth is to make a big deal about God so much so that the entire world knows who He is and is faced with a decision to worship Him or not.

Furthermore, one of the most practical ways to show "undeserved favor" is by giving to others. When you give money or some other gift to someone, you are demonstrating grace to them because they have done nothing to deserve it. The Bible is clear on giving and doing so with generosity. In the law, there are multiple provisions for the poor and the foreigners in the land. Jesus Himself, says in Acts 20:35 "*It is more blessed to give than receive.*" Giving generously to others should be a regular part of a Christian's life. It is God's remedy for us to not be mastered by money and the act of giving keeps us dependent upon God and not ourselves. Also, giving helps us keep an eternal perspective that stores up treasures in heaven and not treasures on earth that will be destroyed in time. Collectively, giving to others who have need or just blessing someone is an inexplicable action that causes people to be curious as to why you would do such a thing. Their curiosity provides you the opportunity to share with them how you have been shown such a grace gift by God that motivates you to share grace with others. My family and I have seen this first hand since the makeover of our home. Our neighbors around us have all stopped and asked what went on over the weekend. When we tell them of the generosity of our church family, they all marvel at the kindness of our church. The church's generosity is a testimony in our neighborhood and is giving the church a platform to share the message of grace in the Gospel of Jesus Christ.

Christian, be a generous grace giver because of the free gift of grace you have received, and then look for opportunities to share your motivation behind being so generous, the Gospel.

Living Out the Gospel Questions:
1. How do you experience the grace of God on a regular basis?
2. How does it make you feel when someone blesses you with a grace gift? What is your typical response?
3. How often does the idea of God's grace cross your mind? Explain the frequency or infrequency.
4. Would you characterize your life as being full of grace? Why or why not?

Gospel Living

5. How is your church known as a place of grace outside of promoting the Gospel message?
6. How does your life need to change based on what you learned through this chapter?

Chapter 4:

Gospel Lifestyle—Mercy and Forgiveness

"Only those who have learned well to be earnestly dissatisfied with themselves, and to be confounded with shame at their wretchedness truly understand the gospel."[22] John Calvin

      I will never forget walking alongside my friend during his parent's divorce. The news of his father having an affair rocked his world and caused him to question the reality of all he had experienced with his family

---

[22] Haley DiMarco and Michael DiMarco, "Over It: Getting Up and Moving On after Bad Stuff Happens," (Grand Rapids, MI: Revell, 2011), 38.

growing up. He described it like waking up from a 20 yearlong dream. I listened to him express the whirlwind of emotions that he was experiencing-from hurting for his mom, being angry with his dad and at the same time hurting for him, all the while feeling helpless to do anything about it. On the night he found out, he skipped church and drove down to the river to be alone, cry, and process his emotions. There, he knew from God's Word what he needed to do.

His dad was kicked out of the house and living like a nomad in the city trying to figure out his next move. It was during this time that my friend called his dad on the phone. He broke the news to his dad that he had heard about everything that had happened. This news caused his dad to breakdown in tears on the other side of the phone. His dad then confessed to what he had done and asked for his forgiveness. This request for forgiveness was the moment of truth for my friend as a son and, most importantly as a Christian. What would his response be? My friend told me that his mind was already made up. Those words of forgiveness to his dad came a lot easier than he thought, but he explained to me that it was his understanding of the gospel that made his actions of forgiveness easier than normal.

Sadly, his parents were unable to reconcile to one another, but my friend learned a lot in that process though.

Forgiveness is not always a once and done action in our human relationships. Most of the time we have to choose to forgive others over and over again, and we may even have to ask for forgiveness from that person ourselves at some points in the journey.

Not Getting What You Deserved and Giving Up the Right to Get Even

I pair mercy and forgiveness together in this chapter because I believe showing someone forgiveness is oftentimes the mercy that we have to show to someone. So, like the chapter on "Love and Justice" we will take a look at these two attributes and how they work together. Let's begin by defining these two terms.

Mercy is a lot like grace but with a little twist. I have often heard it said that grace is getting something you do not deserve and mercy is not getting what it is that you do deserve. More precisely Millard Erickson defines mercy as God's "tenderhearted, loving compassion for his people. It is his tenderness of heart toward the needy."[23] John Frame adds to that definition by saying, "God's goodness toward those who are in misery."[24] God, in His grace, sees us as sinners deserving of punishment,

---

[23] Millard J. Erickson, "Christian Theology," (Grand Rapids: Baker Academic, 1998), 322.
[24] John M. Frame, "The Doctrine of God," (Phillipsburg: Presbyterian & Reformed, 2002), 437.

but He shows us forgiveness and salvation offered through His Son, Jesus. On the other hand, God in His mercy sees us in our misery and helpless condition of our own making, and He interacts with us so that we do not have to suffer our deserved consequences. One can see how closely related grace and mercy are, which explains why so often grace and mercy are paired together.

Building on Erickson's definition of "loving compassion for his people," we come to understand that God's mercy necessitates a relentless action towards humanity. God's mercy is not something that He just possesses, but it is, at the same time, the very thing that He does. Perhaps an illustration will help explain what I mean. We can flip on the TV and interact with commercials that pull on our heart strings by showing us pictures of children in despicable circumstances. In that moment, sitting in the comforts of our nice houses we have compassion on those children. We have a mercy on them that does not want to see them stay in the misery in which they dwell. But the commercial ends, and our TV programs come back on and we quickly forget that mercy we experienced. God cannot have mercy on people WITHOUT responding in a positive way towards them to relieve them of their misery. The great news is that God has already moved on behalf of the people in the world to free them from their misery by sending His Son, Jesus Christ, to give His life as a ransom and grant them freedom.

God's mercy is not just seen in Jesus' actions on the cross but in the very fact that Jesus is on earth to die on a cross. The mercy of God is His motivation behind providing a way to be forgiven of sin. God did this multiple times throughout Scripture, particularly, with the nation of Israel who as a result of their sin found themselves in undesirable situations of their own doing. The psalmist, Asaph, describes this as he recounts the work of God in the nation of Israel. He says in Psalm 78:38, *"Yet he, being compassionate, atoned for their iniquity and did not destroy them; he restrained his anger often and did not stir up all his wrath."* This verse also gives us understanding as to why He does not destroy everyone who ever walks this earth the very moment they commit their first sin. Still, God holds out mercy to all individuals who remain in sin and who have not received the mercy offered in the free gift of salvation found in Jesus Christ. I am so thankful for the mercy of God and His perfect patience.

Forgiveness is what we all want but do not want to freely give out. It is a term and an action that we are very familiar with, but I still want to define it so we all are on the same page. Forgiveness is not requiring payment or resettlement for a wrong done. Forgiveness contains mercy because a person is not giving an individual what they do deserve. I want to share with you my favorite phrase that John Piper gives to remember what forgiveness is; "forgiveness has the word 'give' in it and not the word 'get.' Forgiveness is not 'getting' even but 'giving' up the right to get even with someone."[25] Let that serve as a reminder to you when you are faced with the decision to forgive.

God makes it very clear throughout the Bible that He freely offers forgiveness of sins to those who repent and believe. Isaiah in 43:25 says, "*I, I am He who wipes out your transgressions for my own sake.*" Let me remind you that there is a major difference between the forgiveness God offers individuals from their sins and the forgiveness that you and I may offer to someone who has wronged us. God in His justice cannot let sin go unpunished. Therefore, God does not just wash over our sins, but they have been justly paid for by Jesus on the cross. Remember that forgiveness costs you nothing, but it cost Jesus His life. Paul reminds his readers of this in Ephesians 1:7 when he says, "*In Him we have redemption through His blood, the forgiveness of our trespasses, according to the riches of His grace.*" Believers have been made right before God because of the sacrifice of Jesus Christ extended to us as a grace gift. With the definitions understood,

---

[25] John Piper, "Fifty Reason Why Jesus Came to Die," (Wheaton, IL: Crossway, 2006), 36.

let's look at an example of mercy and forgiveness found in the Scriptures.

70 X 70

The clearest example of mercy and forgiveness in Scripture is found in a parable in Matthew 18. The parable is Jesus' response to a question asked by Peter. While the text is lengthy, I think it is necessary to include in its entirety so you can read through it.

"Then Peter came up and said to him, "Lord, how often will my brother sin against me, and I forgive him? As many as seven times?" Jesus said to him, "I do not say to you seven times, but seventy-seven times. "Therefore, the kingdom of heaven may be compared to a king who wished to settle accounts with his servants. When he began to settle, one was brought to him who owed him ten thousand talents. And since he could not pay, his master ordered him to be sold, with his wife and children and all that he had, and payment to be made. So, the servant fell on his knees, imploring him, 'Have patience with me, and I will pay you everything.' And out of pity for him, the master of that servant released him and forgave him the debt. But when that same servant went out, he found one of his fellow servants who owed him a hundred denarii, and seizing him, he began to choke him, saying, 'Pay what you owe.' So, his fellow servant fell down and pleaded

with him, 'Have patience with me, and I will pay you.' He refused and went and put him in prison until he should pay the debt. When his fellow servants saw what had taken place, they were greatly distressed, and they went and reported to their master all that had taken place. Then his master summoned him and said to him, 'You wicked servant! I forgave you all that debt because you pleaded with me. And should not you have had mercy on your fellow servant, as I had mercy on you?' And in anger his master delivered him to the jailers, until he should pay all his debt. So also, my heavenly Father will do to every one of you, if you do not forgive your brother from your heart."

    Here Peter approaches Jesus to ask how many times he should forgive someone. In the Jewish law it was customary to forgive up to 3 times, so Peter thought he was being super generous when he suggested 7 times. He was shocked that Jesus told him that our forgiveness should be limitless, or that we should forgive without keeping count. Jesus then shares this parable of how ridiculous it is for us as believers to not forgive because of how much we have been forgiven by God.

    The parable is of a king who wants to settle accounts with all people who owe him money. One man owes him an unpayable debt. It is the equivalent of about 6 billion dollars today. The king issues out a justifiable punishment that would satisfy the king. But the man gets down on his knees and begs for him to have patience with him because he will pay it all back. This is where the king shows his greatest mercy (he had already been showing mercy by letting the debt go unsettled) because he sees the servant's desperate situation and knows that he will never be able to pay that money back. The king wants to meet the servant's needs, and he does so by forgiving him of his debt. This demonstrates a great picture of the mercy found in the Gospel because we owe a debt we could never repay, but in crying out to God for forgiveness we can receive forgiveness we do not deserve. Next, this servant goes out and finds a man who owes him money and begins to choke him. This man owed the servant the equivalent of about $12,000 in today's terms. Obviously, this servant did not learn a thing about the mercy and forgiveness that he received as he had the man thrown into jail until he could repay all of the debt. Someone informed the king of the forgiven servant's actions, and the king put him in jail.

    I think we easily look at this situation and think how wicked this man was to be forgiven so much and then not forgive someone who owed him a lesser debt. But we are just as wicked when we choose not to forgive or hold a grudge against someone for what they did. You say, "How is that so?" It is so because God has forgiven us so much. He is the "king" in that parable. The problem is either we truly do not see ourselves as wicked and forgiven by God or that we are so self-centered that we expect to be treated differently than we treat others, and we take for granted the mercy and forgiveness that God has shown us. It is hard for me to say this but I am fully convinced of this truth: *There is no room for unforgiveness in the Christian life*. I realize I do not know your situation and all that you have gone through. I have never experienced your hurt, abuse, or scars. However, I am convinced through this Scripture and when we grasp an eternal perspective, Jesus is saying "Child of mine you have been forgiven so much by God that there is nothing that can be done on this earth that will out do the forgiveness given to you that you did not deserve, so forgive others."

We Died Before We Came Here

When I came to the church where I am currently serving, I knew of a missionary family in the church that had suffered great tragedy. I had this message of Gospel Living on my mind to teach pretty quickly to the students because I think it is essential for every Christian to know and live out. The mother of this family that experienced the tragedy quickly came to mind for this topic of mercy and forgiveness. After doing some asking around to see if it would be appropriate for me to ask her, I got affirmatives from everyone and immediately asked her to sit down and do a video explaining their journey and what happened. She and her late husband along with their four kids went to serve in North Africa as missionaries in a Muslim country. They started helpful and legitimate agencies that served the local prisons and gave micro loans to former prisoners to help them start businesses to supply for their families. The work they did was even recognized by the local government and was greatly appreciated. At the same time, they openly lived out their faith and made the Gospel known with wisdom to the people they worked with and served. Over time some false allegations came up in the local newspaper about them paying individuals off to become Christians. After a few falsified stories like these and brief retractions made after confrontation, their well-known presence in the country made them a target for Al-Qaida. One morning, a few Al-Qaida members attempted to kidnap the husband. The husband was a big man and resisted these three individuals until one of them pulled a gun out and shot him in the head. The mother goes on to share how their life was turned upside down that day, but that through the haze of all that was going on she cried out to God and said "You have to be glorified!" Shortly after this plea, she received an answer from God that "He is glorified," which helped alleviate struggle with the "why" of this event. She went on to share that the only way she could forgive these men was by understanding all that Christ had done in forgiving her. She concluded by saying that, "It is only by the grace of God that we can forgive...and He gives us that grace. But we have to ask for it."

She has since told this story in a book titled, *We Died Before We Came Here* under the name of Emily Foreman that is published by NavPress. It is a great book that I recommend you pick up and read. God has continued to be glorified through this family's testimony of faithfulness to return regularly to continue on their ministry. The community and government officials have welcomed them and encouraged them to continue their work. Even the son has gotten to sit down with one of the men who shot his father and extend forgiveness to him directly. God does remarkable things through the obedient hearts of His servants who understand the Gospel and practice the aspects of the Gospel, such as forgiveness, in their everyday life.

This is the single greatest example of human forgiveness I have ever seen played out by someone I personally know. To the point I made earlier about forgiveness, it is not a once and done thing as a human. Every return trip to this country is an opportunity for Satan to pick at a wound; therefore, each temptation must be squashed not by sheer will power but by the overwhelming reality and forgiveness extended through the Gospel of Jesus Christ. God is glorified in the obedience of His people who respond in action by showing the same love, justice, grace, mercy, and forgiveness demonstrated to them by God. Our lives of obedience provide us the platform to share the Gospel and be heard.

Applying Mercy and Forgiveness to Life Until It Becomes a Lifestyle

The clear and obvious application of mercy and forgiveness leads to potentially the hardest thing we may have to do in life and that is FORGIVE someone. While I could give a long list of health benefits that psychologists say come along with forgiving others, I think forgiving someone for those reasons alone is self-seeking. Any self-seeking motivation in this life will at some point break down and will no longer suffice. Remember, forgiving another human being for the wrong that they have done to you is often not a one-time event. If your motivation is self-seeking, what happens when you did not experience that desired emotion you hoped to receive when you forgave that person? Odds are great that you will be back to square one with unforgiveness and possibly an increased amount of bitterness.

However, when the motivation of our forgiveness comes not from a self-seeking emotion but a loving exhortation from the One who has forgiven us, that reality never changes and will remain the same even the hundredth time we have to forgive someone. As I write this application down, I pray for You, the reader, that God would give you a glimpse of the magnitude of forgiveness that He has shown you, so you can find the right motivation to forgive whoever it is that needs to be forgiven.

On a practical level, giving forgiveness is not always easy. There are always those individuals who have no idea that they hurt you or even those people who do not care that they hurt you. My encouragement to you is always verbalize forgiveness to someone face-to-face. Of course, use wisdom and caution to keep yourself safe. If face-to-face is not possible then a phone call or a letter could be used. You may never know how God might use that to convict their heart of sin and draw them to Himself.

For others of you, the individual who has wronged you may be deceased or unreachable. This is where you go before God in prayer and forgive them. The appropriate response in the area of forgiveness is that you do your part. You cannot control how the other person responds, so just do what God has convicted you to do and trust Him with the results. Experience the freedom that comes when you give up the right to get even with someone else.

Jonathan Kyle

    An application that is specific to mercy would be that you become a person of action. Remember the illustration about starving children on a commercial? Well, the appropriate response when God fills you with mercy and compassion about a certain situation, person, or a group of people is to respond in some way. Know that when God grants you mercy, He is not content with you just feeling sorry for the person. God wants that mercy to move us to do something about their condition. When you see a homeless person on the streets in your town, get involved with your church's benevolence team or a local nonprofit organization meeting the needs of the poor. Give regularly, serve consistently, and be patient with those you serve alongside by listening to them and their stories. True and authentic mercy most often will lead to genuine relationships that are ongoing. Anytime that you seek to serve someone out of compassion and mercy it will cost you your time, your abilities, and your resources. Embrace the need to establish relationships with those who are hurting and do not be content with meeting a need from a distance. With that in mind, avoid handouts that meet an immediate and physical need that may enable them to continue in their current state. Instead, evaluate the skill set of the person and assist them to see the value they bring to the relationships around them. Read books like *When Helping Hurts* by Steve

Gospel Living

Corbett and Brian Fikkert. Be a listening ear to those who are in obvious need. Let your mercy move you to action. The Gospel demands it!

Living Out the Gospel Questions
1. Is there someone you need to forgive right now?
2. Why do we struggle with grasping how much God has forgiven us?
3. Why is acting upon our mercy so hard?
4. What are some ways that you can be merciful daily with the people you are around?
5. How can showing mercy and forgiveness be a platform for you to share the Gospel?

Jonathan Kyle

Chapter 5:

Gospel Lifestyle-Humility and Service

"The Gospel should be presented as bigger than salvation, more robust than go to heaven when one dies, and more pressing than just at the time of conversion…a missional renaissance requires seeing the gospel not as merely the entry fee to Christianity but as the currency of the Christian life."[26]

Throughout my whole life I have been thrust into leadership roles in the areas of

---

[26] *Ed Stetzer, "Exegete Your Culture: 10 Checkpoints for Knowing and Reaching Your Culture" Ed Stetzer & Mission Group, 2016 Wheaton IL.*

influence that God has given me. No doubt, early on in my life I sought out these roles and forced myself into many of them. However, as I have gotten older, I have decided I would much rather sit back and let others lead than to take the reins myself. To borrow a line from Spiderman's uncle Ben with my own twist on it, I would say, "With roles of leadership come great responsibilities." With many responsibilities comes a great amount of giving an account to God for what I have or have not done. Therefore, it is much easier being the person who just takes orders and serves the person in leadership.

In leadership, my number one principle is "never ask anyone to do something that you are not willing to do yourself." There is no job that is too below you, and you are never too far above the people that you serve. This principle has helped me evaluate the question I think all pastors must ask themselves, "Do I really love the people that I lead?" The leader is the greatest servant. In other words, to lead someone means that you actually serve them. The greatest servant is the greatest leader. Look around in our society and in our world and that is not the picture that is being painted by most leaders in the spotlight. Therefore, when we evaluate the leaders in our lives, we are often skeptical and wonder whether or not we are just pawns being manipulated in the leader's game so that he or she can accomplish what he wants to do in life. There is so much abuse of power and of leadership that we find it too good to be true when we find a leader in our lives who honestly wants to serve us and wants to help us reach our greatest good. But that is exactly what we find in the Bible: the greatest man and leader to ever walk this earth says, "For even the Son of Man came not to be served but to serve, and to give his life as a ransom for many" (Mark 10:45). In the area of leadership, one the greatest things that I love about Jesus is that He never asked anyone to do something that He was not willing to do Himself. When the Master and Savior of our lives calls us to do something with humility we MUST obey and serve Him not out of duty but out of love, appreciation, and admiration for our leader who willingly humbled Himself and served us on the cross.

Humility is Needed for Service

Humility is a word that is easy to define but very difficult to practice. Whether or not we will surrender in obedience to Christ begins with the choice of humility. With that said, humility as it is used in the Old Testament, was often associated with the poor and afflicted, as in 2 Samuel 22:28 that says, "*You save a humble people but your eyes are on the haughty to bring them down.*" These are the words of a song of David after he had been delivered by God from his enemies. This idea is communicated in other places in the Old Testament like Psalms 138:6, Proverbs 3:34 and 29. Continually, this promise of God served as an encouragement for those who honored God and sought to live in submission to it helped them to know that He saw their condition and would take care of them despite their current circumstances. At the same time, it served as a warning to the prideful enemies of God's people who like Nebuchadnezzar thought they were responsible in their own strength for their temporary success. The point is that those who had humility often demonstrated it through their recognition of their sinful condition before a holy God, their obedience to God, and their submission to Him.[27]

In the New Testament the word is very similar to how we would view the word today. Humility is demonstrated by a person who refuses to look down on others (Matt. 18:4). It is also characterized by someone who is not overly concerned about their social status (Matt. 23:12). Overall, the definition of humility is found in Paul's use of what is believed to be an early hymn found in Philippians 2:5-11. *"[T]hough he was in the form of God, did not count equality with God a thing to be grasped" (vs. 6).* This verse always blows me away in how Christ demonstrates both "meekness" (controlled

---

[27] Gary Hardin, *The Holman Illustrated Bible Dictionary*, 1st Ed. (2003) Nashville: Holman Bible Publishers, "Humility."

strength) and humility. Jesus is fully God; therefore, He possesses all the power of God in human flesh. However, Jesus never takes advantage of that dynamic power for His own interest or convenience, but only uses that power for the good of others and the ultimate glory of God. Christ's example here is almost unfathomable to us as humans because in our sinfulness we seek to take advantage of our finite power in order for it to be advantageous for us. While that is not always a bad thing, we see it falls greatly short of the standard set for us by our Savior in how He constantly humbled Himself and served others.

Keep reading in the next verse, and it says, *"but made himself nothing, taking the form of a servant, being born in the likeness of men."* I cannot read this verse without hearing the echoing of the words of a chorus by a band called Downhere that says,

"How many kings step down from their thrones

How many lords have abandoned their homes?

How many greats have become the least for me?

And how many gods have poured out their hearts

To romance a world that is torn all apart

How many fathers gave up their sons for me?

Only one did that for me."[28]

This similar storyline may capture the hearts of romantics who love to read or watch stories unfold on the screen of royalty falling in love with a commoner. However, even in the movies and my limited knowledge of romance movies, I do not know many story lines where the royalty gives his life for the common person of his kingdom. The work of Jesus and the humility that it takes for Him to take on the flesh of humanity is a humility that we cannot grasp. Think about it, the limitless God that exists outside of all creation is now confined to a body of flesh and bone. The One who spoke into existence all of creation, now takes on the form of what He created. He who would and is now sitting at the right hand of God left the throne room of Heaven to walk among sin tarnished creation. It is not just that Jesus became flesh; it is that he, the Always, Eternal One voluntarily stepped into death-His own judgement on sin! This move radiates humility!

As if the last two verses were not humbling enough, verse 8 says, "*And being*

---

[28] "How Many Kings," 2008, CD, track 13, Downhere, *Ending is Beginning*, Centricity Music, 2010.

Gospel Living

found in human form, he humbled himself by BECOMING OBEDIENT TO THE POINT OF DEATH (emphasis mine), even death on a cross." Jesus even willingly gives Himself up to be put to death on a humiliating cross. In the middle of that verse, we find the key to humility. Obedience. Who was Christ obedient to? He was obedient to the Father, God. Humility is obedience. Humility is hearing the ultimate authority of all of life, God the Creator, and choosing to respond obediently to His command. Therefore, every action of obedience to God is driven by the belief that God's way is best. While humility is not often the word that comes to your mind when you think of the Gospel, know that it is Christ's humility or obedience to the Father that paves the way for salvation. Humanly speaking, humility, obedience, or surrender is a necessary component to receive salvation by faith. One must have humility to acknowledge their sin and repent of it. One must have humility to recognize they cannot save themselves and place their faith in Jesus Christ for salvation. One must have humility to say "No" to their flesh the rest of their life, and then say "Yes" to God receiving His instruction as the best way.

Remember that at the root of the word "humility" is the word "humble." Is it said about you that you are "humble?" Do you recognize that everything you have that is good is from God and is undeserved? If we look at the two verses that come just before the Philippians 2:5-11 passage, we can see what being "humble" looks like. Philippians 2:3-4 says, "Do nothing from selfish ambition or conceit, but in humility count others more significant than yourselves. Let each of you look not only to his own interest, but also to the interests of others." If we are going to seek to live lives of humility, then we must begin with putting others before ourselves and looking out for the interests of others and not just our own.

The Gospel causes us to be full of humility because we realize we do not deserve salvation but instead punishment. Everything we have is a blessing from God. This place of right standing is like being in a place where you are not supposed to be, but someone special invites you in and you gain entrance on their credentials. In that case, you are truly honored to be there.

On the surface, service is performing a task on behalf of another person or God. As Christians however, in light of the Gospel, all service is done for the glory of God and at its core is worship. Remember every action of obedience to God is driven by belief that God's way is best. If that is the case, then every act of service in our life to God is an act of worship because we are responding to Him in obedience, ultimately saying "He knows best." Understanding service as worship then gives insight to people like myself who always struggled with why churches called their Sunday gathering a

"Worship Service." These gatherings are service because when believers gather to pray, sing, listen, and hopefully apply the truth of God's Word to life until it becomes a lifestyle, they are presenting acts of service to God or in their actions they are declaring God is worthy.

I have linked these two aspects of the Gospel, humility and service, together because a person will not serve someone for the glory of God unless he first puts that individual before himself and considers their needs as greater than his own. Paul expresses this idea clearly of how the love of Jesus for lost humanity served as the motivation for the giving of His life on the cross in Romans 5:6-8 that says *"For while we were still weak, at the right time Christ died for the ungodly. For one will scarcely die for a righteous person—though perhaps for a good person one would dare even to die--- but God shows his love for us in that while we were still sinners, Christ died for us."* Paul is exactly right in saying "*one will SCARCELY die for a righteous person.*" I understand dying for someone compared to serving them may be a little extreme; however, I would argue that the same requirement of putting the other person's needs before your own is required in both instances, just at different levels. Therefore, in order to serve someone for the glory of God, we must either be motivated out of love for them, or be motivated out of love and appreciation for our Savior who first served us by giving those who believe abundant life.

In the New Testament and in Paul's writings the idea of service carries with it the idea of "slave labor done for Christ's sake."[29] The New Testament writers would use the word "bondservant" to communicate their status before God. While there may be several different words used, the word "dulos" is common which means "devoted to another to the disregard of one's own interests."[30] Paul encapsulates this best in Galatians 2:20 when he writes, "*I have been crucified with Christ. It is no longer I who live, but Christ who lives in me. AND THE LIFE I NOW LIVE in the flesh I LIVE BY FAITH* (emphasis mine) *in the Son of God, who loved me and gave himself for me.*" Paul understands what many people who call themselves "Christians" do not. If I have received forgiveness from an unpayable debt that I owed, then my life does not belong to me anymore but to the One who paid my debt. As Christians, we should live in humble servanthood to our Lord out of the overflow of gratitude in our heart for the new life that was given to us. Galatians 2:20 describes why the Gospel DEMANDS of us to be servants of Christ and subsequently servants of others for His glory. Now, let's take a look

---

[29] Steve W. Lemke, *The Holman Illustrated Bible Dictionary*, 1st Ed. (2003) Nashville: Holman Bible Publishers, "Service."
[30] "What is a Bondservant," Bondservant, March 23, 2020, http://thebondservant.org/?page_id=68

at some examples from Scripture in how humility was required for service to take place.

The Humblest Person on the Face of the Earth

Be careful when you hear someone make the claim "I am a humble person." One should be very cautious then when someone says "I am the humblest person on the face of the earth." The phrase is usually an oxymoron. One cannot make that boast and at the same time be true to their claim. Can they? Let's take a look at the book of Numbers which is written by Moses and explore a comment he makes to this end and see if it is possible for a person to justifiably make this claim.

In Numbers chapter 12, the authority of Moses is challenged by none other than his own brother and sister, Aaron and Miriam. Moses' siblings opposed him because he was married to a Cushite woman. No doubt, this was racially motivated. A Cushite was a reference to someone of Ethiopian descent. Her appearance would have been that of a native African. Their disdain for Moses' wife caused them to call into question his supreme authority, and concluded that God could just as well speak to and through them. Verse 3 then says, "*Now the man Moses was very MEEK, more than all people who were on the face of the earth."* The word "meek" in this verse is mostly translated "humble" or even "poor." This self-designation may have been out of line, if it were not for what happened next. God summons all three of them into the "Tent of Meeting" and descends upon the tent in the form of a cloud. God clarifies how He is the One who gives prophets words to speak. This typically happens through a vision. However, that is not the case for Moses as God speaks to him face to face. God then strikes Miriam with leprosy. Aaron turns immediately to Moses and says, *"Oh, my lord, do not punish us because we have done foolishly and have sinned" (11).*

What happens next takes a huge dose of humility and proves that Moses deserves the nomenclature "humblest man on the face of the earth." Have you ever been disrespected or had your authority challenged? Typically, what is produced inside of you is not humility but more like pride that leads to a vengeful spirit. I would expect Moses to respond with "No! She is going to get what she deserves for challenging my authority and simultaneously challenging God's authority." Instead, he humbles himself and has compassion on his sister. In humility, Moses serves his sister by speaking on her behalf to God and pleads with God for her healing by saying, *"O God, please heal her—please."* How can someone do that? Moses knows that he is unworthy of the position that he has been given by God, and even though his sister deserves punishment, he remembers his humble position and asks God to give her something she doesn't deserve, her life and health back. I am blown away at this humble servant who was attacked by the very people he loves, yet he desires their wellbeing. This is putting someone else's need above your own and doing your part to help meet their need.

The Greatest Leader is the Greatest Servant

The natural thing that seems to happen in groups that spend time together is to determine the pecking order of everyone's position in the group. The one who typically gets to be the leader or person of the highest priority is the one who declares "I am the leader" first. I see this regularly with my kids as they play with their friends in the yard. Someone has an idea for a new game to play, and one kid immediately declares that they will be in charge. Sometimes this self-proclamation goes without disagreement, but other times it leads to a stalemate that prevents the game from ever taking place. In Mark chapter 10, we find a similar scenario.

James and John come to Jesus to request *"Grant us to sit, one on your right hand, and one on your life, in your glory." (37)* Jesus asks them if they can suffer like He will suffer, and they correctly answer "yes."

Jesus then tells them that it is not His position to grant those requests. Then, like the children in my yard, the other ten disciples get upset at James and John for making such a request for places of priority. Jesus then calls them all together and says, "*You know that those who are considered rulers of the Gentiles lord it over them, and their great ones exercise authority over them. But it shall not be so among you. But whoever would be great among you must be your servant, and whoever would be first among you must be slave of all.*" (42-44) This teaching of Jesus is not only a great leadership maxim but it is directed at His disciples in how they are to treat everyone when He said, "*whoever would be first among you must be SLAVE OF ALL.*" The next phrase that comes out of Jesus' mouth probably floors His disciples. In verse 45, He says, "*For even the Son of Man came not to be served BUT TO SERVE and give his life as a ransom for many.*" The person who deserved highest priority does not demand the elevated position, but instead, He has come to serve. Jesus is clear on how He intends to serve and that is through dying on the cross to "*give his life as a ransom for many.*"

Undoubtedly, Jesus' work on the cross is a magnificent example of humility and service, but there is another example that He gives that communicates humility through the act of serving. After making arrangements to observe the Passover with His disciples, Jesus gets up in the middle of the meal and does something unexplainable in their culture. In John 13:3-15, we read of how Jesus takes on the role typically given to the lowest of non-Jewish slaves. Moreover, Jesus even takes on the appearance of a slave by removing His outer garment and tying a towel around His waist. He proceeds to wipe the dirt, grime, and toe jam off of His disciple's feet and then dries their feet with the towel around His waist.

    He completes the service of washing all of their feet then He sits down with them and explains what He has done. Jesus tells them that they are right to call Him "Lord" and "Master," but He informs them that as a follower of Him no one is above the other one as He explained in Mark 10. His actions demonstrate true humility that leads to service. Jesus gave up His rights to be served as their Master and served them instead. The command that He then gives to the disciples is not that they go around washing everyone's feet, but that they would go around giving up their right to be served in order to serve others. This is the same call for every follower of Christ today: humble yourself and serve others without prejudice.

Jonathan Kyle

Paying The Ultimate Sacrifice-The Four Chaplains

Throughout history there are ample examples of people who paid the ultimate sacrifice, giving of their life, in order to serve and meet the needs of others around them. However, I came across this story of four chaplains that struck my attention in how they served in a very simple and discreet way that could have gone unnoticed if someone had not perpetuated their story.

The year was 1943, and it is in the dead of winter, February 3rd. The USS Dorchester was carrying 905 servicemen through the North Atlantic. For some reason, the ship left its convoy just a few hours before reaching its destination. Unbeknownst to them, they were being stalked by a German submarine who fired a torpedo right at the ship's stern. The torpedo ended up striking the middle of the ship and exploded in the middle of the boiler room. A great number of servicemen died immediately in the explosion, and many others were trapped below the deck. Fast asleep, hundreds of other soldiers were flung from their bunks, and in a daze of both sleep and adrenaline rush sought to find their way to the deck. With the ship taking on water rapidly, the ship began to roll starboard. Adding to all of these difficulties was their inability to send distress flares to call escort vessels that were not too far off because of security reasons. In the icy water, the overcrowded lifeboats began to capsize, and in the chaos, rafts were drifting away without anyone in them.

On the deck were four Army chaplains; George L. Fox, Alexander D. Goode, Clark V. Poling, and John P. Washington. Amidst the terror and fear, these men moved around the ship to help calm the frightened men, directing the shocked soldiers to lifeboats and handing out life jackets calmly to the men who passed by without them. Quickly, the life jackets were all gone, yet four young soldiers, terrified and without life vests, stood waiting to be given one. Without hesitation, the chaplains removed their life vests and forced them upon these young soldiers.

These four chaplains gave away their only means of saving themselves so that the four men could be saved. The story goes that as men were rowing away from the sinking ship in lifeboats, they looked back to see the four chaplains on the tilting deck, linked together with their arms and their heads bowed in prayer to the God in whom they loved and served. These four humble and self-sacrificing chaplains plunged to their death in the icy cold waters of the North Atlantic along with 675 other servicemen.[31]

---

[31] Emmy French, "No Greater Glory: The Four Chaplains and the Sinking of the USAT Dorchester," Army History, March 26, 2020. https://armyhistory.org/no-greater-glory-the-four-chaplains-and-the-sinking-of-the-usat-dorchester/

This story summons tears to my eyes as I think about the intentional sacrifice that they made to serve four men. From observation, acts of valor, sacrifice, and service on a day-to-day practical level do not happen by accident. They happen because men and women make it a discipline and priority to put other people before themselves. Then they live their life looking for and noticing opportunities to serve, and they seize those opportunities when they arise. Acts of humility, service, and sacrifice are not uniquely Christian traits, but for someone who understands the humility and sacrifice of Jesus Christ to provide their salvation, they must make it a priority and a normal way of life.

Applying Humility and Service to Life Until it Becomes a Lifestyle

I remember vividly my response to a question that was asked of me in a search team interview for my first job as a student pastor. The man turned to me and asked something similar to this, "What is the greatest act of service that Jesus did while on this earth?" For whatever reason I quickly responded with "When Jesus washed the feet of His disciples." I then spent 2-3 minutes explaining my answer. It was later, as I was replaying the interview in my head, that I slapped myself on the forehead because I believe the answer the man was probably looking for was Jesus' sacrificial death on the cross. If I could answer the question again, I would definitely say it was Jesus' death on the cross. However, I am still blown away by the Lord of the universe, the Teacher, who was not above washing the feet of his students. If He gave us that example, then we should humble ourselves to serve even those who may be deemed "lowly" in our society.

    Therefore, you, His disciple, should never think you are above serving anyone on this earth. You might say, "But you don't know what this person has done?" I would say to you, "You're right! I don't know but Jesus knew that Judas would betray Him to death and he still washed his feet." In other words, Jesus knows what you are going through. There may be another excuse that you have like "But this person has had everything handed to them and has no need for money. Why should I serve them?" Remember that Jesus loved and dined with the tax collectors who had all they ever wanted because of their dishonest treatment of their fellow countrymen. Or we could say, "But this person is filthy and disgusting." Remember that Jesus went to the marginalized and outcast of society like lepers and beggars. Some of the greatest witnesses to the Gospel in history have been Christians who stepped up in times of crisis to serve and love those who were considered untouchable or expendable.

Jonathan Kyle

The goal for every follower of Christ is the humility of Christ that understands that no one is below or above me when it comes to serving them. We must think of others before ourselves and do intentional things to remind us of that through everyday practical things like letting other people go before us in line. Or, if you find yourself in a potluck line (sorry I'm Baptist and we can't do anything without having food), think of others who are behind you in line and make sure to deny yourself what you want so they have something to eat.

When we make decisions, we should think of how it will affect those around us and not just ourselves. Remember this, you are not entitled to salvation but it was given to you even though you did not deserve it. Do not think you deserve or are entitled to things on this earth, but think of how you can meet the needs of others. If we can remove the thought "I deserve this" from our regular thinking, then I believe we will more likely put other needs before our own and humbly serve them before ourselves.

Living Out the Gospel Questions
1. In your opinion, what makes a person humble? What needs to change in your life for those things to be true in your life?
2. Who is a model to you of humility and service? What attributes of

their life could you seek to emulate?
3. What are some things you can do today to intentionally serve others?
4. What are some barriers in your life personally to serving others (not aware, too busy, personal pride, don't know what to do, etc.)?
5. List 2-3 everyday practical steps in your life to practice humility and service (holding doors for people, being last in line, being the first to clean up after a meal, etc.).

Chapter 6:

Gospel Lifestyle-Peace and Patience

"The gospel creates a new kind of obedience. Not one of being beaten into it, but because I WANT TO."-J.D. Greear

As I write this chapter, I am sitting at home in the midst of a fourteen-day quarantine since I have just returned from the Dominican Republic on a mission trip. That is right, I am writing in the midst of the COVID19 pandemic that will undoubtedly be a memorable moment in world history. While there are definitely aspects of the quarantine that are nice: spending every day with my family, and having nothing to do because everything is shut down it can create a little cabin fever and desire for social interaction. In the big picture, this is a slight inconvenience for me that is hoping to bring about a greater solution of stopping the spread of this virus.

I bring this up because "peace" is not the pervading emotion that most of the world is experiencing at the current moment. While we are only two weeks into this pandemic the growing sentiment right now is that of fear. Everyone's sense of current safety and future security is being infringed upon as our government officials are urging everyone to stay in their homes to avoid getting the virus or spreading it. Unemployment is the highest it has been in recent history, just after reaching its lowest percentage, and the stock market looks more like a roller coaster that is experiencing more lows than highs. Those who put their trust in the things of this world have a heightened sense of anxiety and concern for not only the future of our country but their individual future.

The isolation that this quarantine is producing has caused many to grow impatient with staying inside and away from each other. The instruction is to endure and wait because the quarantine will only be temporary. But as days turn into weeks and weeks into months, the patience of those willingly staying at home has and is wearing thin.

When we define patience, we will discover that it is more than just waiting.

Jonathan Kyle

"Patience" is more like what is being asked of all Americans right now, be willing to do what is uncomfortable to you with endurance for not only your good but also the good of others. Hopefully, through this introduction you are starting to see how peace and patience fit into the Gospel picture, and, therefore, should be a part of our lives as Christians when we seek to apply the Gospel to life until it becomes a lifestyle.

It Means More Than What You Think

Growing up as a child of the 80's and 90's I heard a lot of talk about peace and learned pretty quickly how to form the symbol for peace with my fingers. I remember President Reagan calling for the tearing down of the Berlin Wall, and then in the early 90's receiving nightly updates on the news of what was happening in the Gulf War. I realize my experience is not unique as many generations had their own crises and wars that caused cries for peace. Since this is typically how we hear the word peace used, our constructed definition has something to do with "the absence of conflict." In the Bible, the word at its very least means that but it also has a much more robust meaning.

Many of us are probably familiar with the word used in the Old Testament for peace. It is the word "Shalom." The word carries with it the idea of completeness or wholeness and deals more with a debt being

Gospel Living

repaid or a vow that is fulfilled in order to restore completeness in a broken relationship. I like to think of the word like a warm fluffy blanket wrapped around a person because it inspires the sense that all is well in the world.

In the New Testament, the word for peace is found in every book except 1 John. The word in its very simple usage is "the absence of war." However, the word took on a greater meaning when the Hebrew Old Testament was translated into Greek. Then it came to mean "a condition and sense of being safe and secure."[32]

When the word peace comes to the Gospel, the term brings to mind all that Christ accomplished on the cross and through His resurrection. His death and resurrection ended the dominance of sin over a person's life and provided a right relationship with God and humanity by grace through faith. In fact, the Gospel can be referred to as the "Gospel of peace" (Eph. 6:15).

A great text that spells this out is Romans 5:1-2 that says, *"Therefore, since we have been justified by faith, we have peace with God through our Lord Jesus Christ. Through him we have also obtained access by faith into this grace in which we stand, and we rejoice in the hope of the glory of God."* From this text we understand that

---

[32] E. Ray Clendenen, *The Holman Illustrated Bible Dictionary*, 1st Ed. (2003) Nashville: Holman Bible Publishers, "Peace."

through the faith of a believer who trusts that Christ has taken their place on the cross and received the just penalty for sin on their behalf, they have been declared right before God as if they had never offended Him in the first place by their sin. And since they have been justified, there is no conflict that exists between them and God, nor will there be any conflict in the future because the sacrifice was eternal. Therefore, they, as believers, have ultimate peace with God because of the life, death, burial, and resurrection of Jesus Christ.

Furthermore, a follower of Christ now has been given grace (something undeserved) in having eternal life and oneness with God. This peace that now exists, given through Christ, gives them hope which is a confident expectation that they will spend eternity with God in heaven.

Have you ever noticed a friend or family member who is in conflict with someone else but in some way, it feels like they are in conflict with you because of how hateful they treat you and talk to you? Their brokenness in one relationship causes them to be in conflict in other relationships. This is true with all of humanity. The reason is because there exists a brokenness in relationship with God and a lack of "shalom" in their life. But, through the reception of the Gospel into our lives and the reconciling of our relationship with God, they are given the peace they need to live at peace with one another. Whether or not they choose to work towards peace depends upon how willing they are to let the Gospel shape their thoughts, attitudes, and actions.

The book of Ephesians is rich with this language of peace and how Christ has provided peace for all of those who believe. In chapter 2, Paul reminds his audience that they were *"dead in the trespasses and sins..."* (2:1). In verse 11, he tells his Gentile audience to remember that at one point they were *"separated from Christ, alienated from the commonwealth of Israel and strangers to the covenants of promise, having NO HOPE and WITHOUT GOD in the world"* (12). This description is very bleak and communicates the harsh reality of those who live in submission to sin and without peace with God. Paul goes on to explain that Christ has provided for them the opportunity to be brought close to God through Christ's blood. Verse 14 is the crux of this understanding of peace in the Gospel as Paul writes, *"For he [Christ] himself is our PEACE* (emphasis mine)*, who has made us both one and has broken down in his flesh the dividing wall of hostility."* Jesus has given those who receive salvation oneness with God by destroying the conflict or hostility that existed between them and God because of sin. Moreover, Jesus brings "peace" between, in this context, the Jews and Gentiles. That means through Jesus one can have peace with everyone because of the peace purchased for them through the blood of Jesus Christ. Peace is then offered as an alluring attraction to the Gospel as Paul says of Christ, *"he came and preached peace to you who were far off and peace to those who were near"* (17). The attraction of the Gospel is to have "peace" with the Creator God and to have peace with others.

Furthermore, two chapters later Paul reminds his readers that they should "walk in a manner worthy of the calling to which you have been called" (4:1). Paul is appealing to the cross of Jesus Christ as the source of their power to now walk, or live, in such a way that is in congruence with the Gospel or the calling they have received from Christ to pursue holiness. This is really the appeal of this book you are holding that the power of what Christ accomplished on the cross should empower you to live out the attributes of the Gospel in your everyday life. If truly you have been changed, given new life through the truth of the Gospel, then walk in accordance with this truth. What are some ways that one can walk in accordance to the truth of God's word? Paul mentions several things here such as; humility, gentleness, patience, bearing with one another in love, and maintaining the unity of the Spirit. Paul then says that they should "*maintain the unity of the Spirit in the bond of peace.*"

Does Paul simply mean here "the absence of conflict?" Anyone who has been in a family for any length of time or involved

Gospel Living

in a church would know there is always going to be conflict at some point in relationships. This means the "bond of peace" must not only mean the absence of conflict but all of the fullness of the definition of peace which can be found in the midst of conflict. The peace referenced here is the promotion of reconciliation like we have seen in the Gospel where one can be safe and secure in their relationship with one another while in disagreement.

If you have ever attempted to reconcile a broken relationship, then you would know that it rarely goes smoothly. What is needed is a commitment to the process of reconciliation and the ability to ask for forgiveness and give forgiveness. That means humility, gentleness, patience, and love must be essential to live at peace and find reconciliation. The great news is that believers now have the power to seek reconciliation and peace as well as a sacrificial example of what it will take to accomplish it. Remember, peace has already been obtained for believers through Jesus Christ, which is freely given by God. Through this peace with God, one has not only obtained a relationship with God but also with His people. Therefore, unity has been given to believers by God through their adoption into the family of God. Paul is then charging believers who have all gained entrance into this family of God to "maintain" the unity through peace. That means it is not only something that they should work towards but it is also something that is WORTH working towards. Peace is essential to unity with other believers because one must be willing to forgive others out of their love and patience with them, and/or when they ask for forgiveness that stems from humility.

Patience is More Than Just Waiting

Anyone who has prayed for patience has learned that they may not like the way in which God grants them patience. God is gracious always to give a believer what they ask for when they ask according to His will, but sometimes He lavishes His grace upon them by giving them what they ask for rather quickly and without having to go through much to obtain it. However, God most commonly gives them what they ask for according to His will by allowing them to receive it through trial. Take an honest look throughout Scripture and you will see both by example and through His directions that He teaches His people and matures them through tests and trials. Patience seems to always be one of those things that when you ask for it, you must go through a trying situation and endure through it before gaining what you asked for, patience.

Patience is more than just waiting. When patience is talked about in Scripture it is most commonly referring to "active endurance of opposition."[33] Frequently one will find this word in connection to encouragement being given to those Christians in the Bible who are undergoing persecution. The encouragement is to endure knowing that God will provide the grace needed to be patient, and that they should wait, trusting that God will get the ultimate victory over their oppressor. With this idea of patience, it may make better sense to use the KJV word "longsuffering." This word in itself gives a better understanding of the true definition.

Another important thing one must understand about patience is that it is not passive. Instead to be patient is to actively engage and being steadfast through the suffering in one's devotion to Christ despite the tribulations in their life. As I said above, trials are what God so often uses in one's life to mature them in their faith. Therefore, to have patience in a trial does not mean one just waits for the trial to pass, but one presses into God as the trial intensifies seeking the blessings that come in their relationship with God and the necessary grace and strength to not only survive but thrive in the trial. All the while, they are walking in faithfulness to the will of God spelled out in the Scripture and not letting the

---

[33] Warren McWilliams, *The Holman Illustrated Bible Dictionary*, 1st Ed. (2003) Nashville: Holman Bible Publishers, "Patience."

difficulty in their life give permission for them to sin.

The book of Romans gives one a good understanding of how God exercised patience as it relates to the sin of all of mankind. In Romans 3, Paul stated the point that "no one is righteous" and that no one will be justified by keeping the law. Paul is building the point that righteousness came from outside of the law, even though all of the Old Testament points to it. Righteousness has come through faith in Jesus Christ. Romans 3:23-26 says, *"for all have sinned and fall short of the glory of God, and are justified by his grace as a gift, through the redemption that is in Christ Jesus, whom God put forward as a propitiation by his blood, to be received by faith. This was to show God's righteousness, because in his DIVINE FORBEARANCE* (emphasis mine) *he had passed over former sins. It was to show his righteousness at the present time, so that he might be just and the justifier of the one who has faith in Jesus."* This is a review of truths that have been covered throughout this book about the Gospel, but I want to slow down with verse 25 that speaks of God's divine forbearance or we might say patience as He had passed over former sins. God actively waited 4,000 years to provide the necessary sacrifice for sins to cover the sins of those who had faith in the coming Messiah so that they may be declared righteous. There is no doubt that God was active throughout the entire 4,000 years between the first sin until the propitiation or the payment satisfying the penalty for sin. He was preparing His people both through prophetic word about the coming Messiah and examples, as simple as the sacrificial system of the Old Testament Law, on how God would bring justice for the millennia of sin for those who place their faith and trust in the coming Messiah. Paul communicates this to explain how God is still holy and just because for those 4,000 years He did not put the full punishment of sin on those people who sinned but received His forgiveness through faith. Paul speaks elsewhere of this perfect patience of God when in Galatians 4:4 he says, "*But when the fullness of time had come, God sent for his Son, born of woman, born under the law, to redeem those who were under the law, so that we might receive adoption as sons.*" God's timing is impeccable as He actively waited to pay the price for sin and provide salvation.

In the same way, God is still patient today as Paul tells us in Romans 2:4, "*Or do you presume on the riches of his kindness and forbearance and patience, not knowing that God's kindness is meant to lead you to repentance?*" God's patience with us today is so that we will repent and have a right relationship with Him. There is patience in the Gospel and there should be patience in those who have received the Gospel.

Jonathan Kyle

Unexpected Patience that Leads to Peace

Many of you know the story of Jacob and Esau. They were twin boys of Isaac (Abraham's promised son). Esau was the oldest son who was known as a hunter and for a less than glamorous feature: he was very hairy. I can relate. On the other hand, Jacob was a momma's boy who stayed in the house and did a lot of cooking. On Isaac's death bed, through the help of his mother, Jacob deceived his ailing father into giving him the blessing reserved for the first-born son, Esau. Then when Esau came in to receive the blessing reserved only for him, Esau was irate to hear that Jacob had deceived his father in stealing his blessing. Genesis 27:38-41 reads, "*Esau said to his father, 'Have you but one blessing, my father? Bless me, even me also, O my father.' And Esau lifted up his voice and wept. Then Isaac his father answered and said to him: 'Behold, away from the fatness of the earth shall your dwelling be, and away from the dew of heaven on high. By your sword you shall live, and you shall serve your brother; but when you grow restless you shall break his yoke from your neck.' Now Esau HATED* (emphasis mine) *Jacob because the blessing with which his father had blessed him, and Esau said to himself, 'The days of mourning for my father are approaching; then I will kill my brother Jacob'.*" Discovering the malicious intent of his brother, Jacob flees to Haran where his mother's brother, Laban, lived. Fast forward 20 years and the blessing from his father, Isaac, has been in full effect for Jacob and he is extremely wealthy. Jacob is leaving his father-in-law to head back towards his homeland and is anticipating a run in with his brother. He makes preparations to bless Esau out of his great wealth with gifts in order to promote peace. Jacob is extremely nervous and fearful that Esau will take his life.

Jacob finally meets Esau and this encounter is recorded in Genesis 33:1-4 that says, *"And Jacob lifted up his eyes and looked, and behold, Esau was coming, and four hundred men with him. So, he divided the children among Leah and Rachel and the two female servants. And he put the servants with their children in front, then Leah with her children, and Rachel and Joseph last of all. He himself went on before them, bowing himself to the ground seven times, until he came near to his brother. But Esau ran to meet him and embraced him and fell on his neck and kissed him, and they wept."* Needless to say, this reunion was not quite what Jacob expected from his brother whom he fled 20 years before because of his threat of murder. After the passing of time, one would only expect to find a bitter older man bent on revenge who has been soured by the thought of what he could have had. Instead, we find a peaceful man who has forgiven his younger brother for his deception and theft of his blessing. On top of that, he refused all of the gifts that Jacob has offered to appease him until Jacob urged and insisted, he take them.

    In the waiting, Esau is able to forgive and be at peace with his estranged brother. This is a rare and supernatural feat because a lapse of time after unresolved conflict often leads individuals to bitterness and rage not patience and peace. This example implies the sensitivity that Esau must have had to the ways of God and the maturity in his faith. It speaks to an active patience that Esau had so he did not just sit around and feel sorry for himself about what had happened in the past, but it shows that he dealt with it before God and continued on in life trusting that if God gave him the chance, he would be at peace enough to show love and forgiveness to his brother. Sadly, Jacob did not return the favor as once again he deceived his brother telling Esau that he would meet him in Seir, but Jacob took off to Succoth. What an amazing testimony of work in Esau's life despite a complete change and appreciation by Jacob of Esau's forgiveness. Believers must have an active patience that works toward peace with others even when they are not around by laying their unresolved bitterness at the feet of Jesus over and over again until they can get to the point of genuine peace with that person.

Gospel Living

Peace With God Promotes Reconciliation with Others

Reconciliation probably deserves a whole chapter in and of itself in this book, but it fits so nicely with peace because Jesus has satisfied a debt owed to God in order to make peace with God and reconcile sinners into a right relationship with Him. The scope of God's reconciliation through Jesus Christ is even bigger than the reconciliation of sinners to God, as grand as that is. Paul encapsulates the enormity of the peace and reconciliation that Jesus brings in a couple of verses in Colossians chapter 1. In a sort of an Ode to Christ and how magnificent He is Paul writes in verses 19-20 *"For in him all the fullness of God was pleased to dwell, and through him to RECONCILE to himself ALL THINGS, whether on earth or in heaven, making PEACE* (emphasis mine) *by the blood of Christ."* In this verse alone one can hear how peace was obtained through Jesus Christ's blood that then provided reconciliation for sinners to God. Notice though that the reconciliation is more than sinful man but it is "all things." What does all things entail?

Paul gives a greater understanding of all things that will be reconciled in Romans 8:19-22 that says, *"For the creation waits with eager longing for the revealing of the sons of God. For the creation was subjected to futility, not willingly, but because of him who subjected it, in hope that the creation itself will be set free from its bondage to corruption and obtain the freedom of the glory of the children of God. For we know that the whole creation has been groaning together in the pains of childbirth until now."* This text makes clear that not only was humanity affected by sin but all of creation is not as it was before The Fall. Therefore, Christ's first coming began the work of reconciliation, namely in humanity, and His second coming will bring to completion the reconciliation of all creation. Still, there is a responsibility that has been given to redeemed humanity in the area of reconciliation.

Paul explains this well in 2 Corinthians chapter 5 that says, *"Therefore, if anyone is in Christ, he is a new creation. The old has passed away; behold, the new has come. All this is from God, who through Christ reconciled us to himself and gave us the ministry of reconciliation."* (5:17-18). Those who have become followers of Jesus Christ have become "new creations" who no longer live for the ways of this world but for the agenda of God.

As recipients of this reconciled relationship, Paul communicates that those who have received reconciliation have also been given the ministry of reconciliation. That means they have been charged with the service of reconciling sinners to God. Let me be clear in what I mean. I am saying that followers of Christ have been entrusted with the responsibility of sharing the Gospel of Peace with others so that they too can be reconciled to God. Like the farmer who sows the seed (Luke 8:4-15) the follower of Christ's task is ONLY to present this Good News to others for a disciple has no ability within themselves to save anyone.

The Bible makes it clear that the only logical conclusion for one who has received peace and reconciliation with the God of the universe is that they would walk this earth representing this Gospel of Peace through Jesus Christ to EVERYONE they encounter and sharing it generously to all. The peace of God and subsequent reconciliation is a life altering truth that must be shared with the nations.

The reconciliation of sinners to God also leads to reconciliation with others. God wants the follower of Christ to live at peace with all people out of the peace that has been given to them through the Gospel. Jesus emphasizes the importance of a person seeking reconciliation with someone who may have something against them before they present their offering before the Lord in Matthew 5:23-26. Again, Jesus speaks of reconciliation but this time if a person has wronged them in Matthew 18:15-18. The process described in this text is what is known as church discipline. While this subject often creates fear or disdain, the process is intended for the person to be at peace with God and with others or in other words to be reconciled. The Gospel of Peace should cause one to "*live peaceably with all*" *(*Romans 12:18b*)* because they have been granted peace with God.

Perfect Timing for Peace

Over the last 15 years of ministry, I have given one week in my summer to working in Clarkston, GA, which is touted as the most diverse square mile in the United States. As a teenager I did work in this city among Muslim refugees mostly from the Middle East. Ever since the city has been designated a refugee city in the US by the United Nations, the city has blossomed with diversity and has become an international city tucked into modern day America. I was introduced to a North American Mission Board missionary named Bennet Ekandem who has been serving there since the turn of the millennia. Our partnership has turned into a friendship of trust and united passion to reach the nations for the Gospel.

One year while serving there, I grew curious as to why so many Burmese people I encountered were Christians. Bennett proceeded to tell me of the account of how Christianity spread to the nation of Burma through one man's obedience to the calling of God. This man is the now famous missionary, Adoniram Judson. Upon hearing generally of how the spread of the Gospel

Gospel Living

took place in Burma, I came home to confirm the validity of the story and found an amazing example of patience and peace.

After several years of living in Burma and suffering much heartache, like the death of several of his kids and eventually his wife, Adoniram got word of a tribe of Animism people called the Karen. In their ancient oral traditions, the story goes that there was an all-powerful God who created the universe. This God created man and eventually woman out of a rib that belonged to man. They believed that as a result of temptation man fell from the grace of God and eventually there would come a Messiah who would bring redemption in connection to this truth, there was a "prophecy that a 'Golden Book' would be returned to them by a white man, and some saw Judson with his Bible as a fulfillment of the prophecy."[34] This was a patient people who waited for some time for the message of peace to be brought to them.

Therefore, Adoniram and a missionary couple and a new Karen believer brought the good news of the Gospel to this tribe in fulfillment of this long-awaited prophecy. Adoniram's tireless work to translate a Bible into the Burmese language and the strategic planting of churches in Burma led to a great many of Burmese coming to faith in Jesus Christ. Now, each

---

[34] J. Stephen Lang, "The Christian History Devotional: 365 Readings and Prayers to Deepen and Inspire Your Faith," (Nashville, TN: Thomas Nelson, 2012), pg. 52.

July there is a great celebration among Baptists called Judson Day. One cannot help but be encouraged by how the Karen people waited patiently in expectation for the answers to their questions to arrive. Actively waiting primed the pump for their immediate embrace of the Gospel of peace.

Applying Peace and Patience to Our Life Until It Becomes a Lifestyle

As a student pastor for over 15 years, I have never observed a more anxious generation than the current generation of students known as Generation Z. In the past, it was common for me to counsel one or two students in a year about stress and anxiety in the privacy of a phone call or in my office. Now, it feels as if every student I know is dealing with a heightened sense of anxiety in their life, and they all speak openly about how they are feeling. There has even been the invention of a new acronym called FOMO (Fear of Missing Out). Students not only have anxiety about the uncertainty of the future or the unsettling reality of the current culture, but they also have anxiety over the possibility that they are missing out on something that COULD BE happening that they do not know about. Numerous reasons exist for why this current generation struggles so greatly with anxiety and I don't pretend to have any quick fixes posed in this book, but the appeal of the Gospel bringing peace is just as much an attraction to people today as it was to the audience the Bible was originally written to who longed for peace as well. Throughout this chapter I hope that you have noticed that the Gospel of Jesus Christ empowers us with the ability to have peace with God and with others and equips us with patience to wait on God to deliver at the perfect time and the ability to have patience with others.

I realize that even right now you may be reading this book and peace is not the word you would use to describe your current state. If that lack of peace is in connection with your relationship with God there are two possible reasons why you do not feel it. First, it could be that you have never fully placed your faith and trust in Jesus Christ as your Savior and Lord who has bridged the gap caused by sin between you and God. If that is the case, I would encourage you to reach out to someone you know who is a follower of Christ or call a local church and ask them how you could receive peace with God.

Second, it could be that you have quit trusting in God for righteousness and have begun trusting in yourself or someone else to make you right with God. If that is the case, I would encourage you to acknowledge your reality before God and return to Him stating your trust in Him alone to grant you peace through Jesus Christ.

Since you have picked up this book and have read this far, I would venture to say that many of you probably understand the peace given to us through Christ with God. If that is the case, most of your issues with peace most likely deal with being at peace with others. The Gospel of peace demands that we live at peace with one another. Practically, you should be a promoter of peace in your relationships with others and simultaneously an encourager to those people to live at peace in their own relationships. That means do not provoke people to anger with your words or actions.

Some people have a gift at provoking people to anger. Having four kids, I see all take their turns at provoking each other to anger. I will never forget when my third son, who was 2 or 3 years old at the time was going through the nightly bedtime routine. I passed by the bathroom and saw him holding a toothbrush, grinning mischievously, and staring at the door waiting for his oldest brother to come into the bathroom. Knowing that his oldest brother gets sick at even the thought of drinking or eating after someone, he was waiting for him to enter the bathroom to pretend like he was using his toothbrush. Now, I know this is a silly and harmless example, but some of us love to do things to get a rise out of people to make them temporarily angry. However, some of us do not know where to draw the line and unknowingly can be pushing people to anger and in effect promote a lack of peace in their relationships.

Gospel Living

Following the instructions of Jesus both in Matthew 5 and 18, the follower of Christ should be sensitive to how they may have offended, harmed, or sinned against someone else and then humble themselves and ask for forgiveness. If they have been sinned against, then they must be bold and honest enough to confront that person in their sin (be wise here and take others with you if it is unsafe) and be quick to forgive them like Esau did Jacob because they realize the undeserved peace granted to them.

Furthermore, believers should be promoters of reconciliation or peace in other people's lives. When someone confides in you about a struggle with someone else, it is really easy for us to choose their side in the conflict. What if we listened attentively, objectively heard the grievance, and instead of assuming maliciousness in the heart of the offender, we assumed an honest mistake or ignorant negligence on the guilty party. Then we would not recommend getting revenge on them but would encourage the person we are talking with to seek reconciliation offering ourselves to go with them to work it out.

If your life is full of conflict, maybe you should take a step back and ask yourself "Am I a promoter of peace or subconsciously a promoter of conflict through jealous or selfish motives?" I have found it always beneficial to ask self-evaluating questions instead of assuming it is someone else's fault. All the while remembering the peace that you have with God and the comfort of being right with Him.

Patience…oh, we do not want to talk about how we could practically apply this. The application of patience could simply be patiently waiting with expectancy in what God wants for you in the future with your life. That means taking the small daily steps of obedience today realizing nothing is wasted with God and what you are doing is preparing you for the future. Working with students reminds me of this often. They cause me to think back to when I was a teenager and time moved slowly. Four years of high school felt like 20 years of my life. I can now understand when they say that they have been praying for something for 6 months and God has not answered and they are feeling frustrated. I remind myself of the patience of God and His impeccable timing, and then I remind them that God's timing is perfect. They must be persistent in their prayers, be active in their obedience to the will of God in His Word, and actively look for how God is answering that prayer all the while trusting God's faithfulness in the past means He will be faithful in the future at just the right time.

There are other more practical steps that you can take to practice patience in your life. The next time you are at the store look for the longest line and hop into it. Many of us do this unknowingly anyways. We hop in what looks like the shortest line until we see

Gospel Living

the line two aisles over moving faster. We switch over to that line only to realize the person who took your spot in the previous line gets through quicker than you. When you put yourself in this longer line, look for the opportunity to engage the people with whom you are standing in line. In the end, we must trust that in your waiting and intentional obedience God is preparing you to intersect someone's life at the perfect time to meet their need at the exact time they are ready to be helped. Remember, God so often grows us in an area we need growth in by giving us a trial that has the potential to produce that needed attribute of the Gospel in us.

Living out the Gospel Questions
1. Personally, what is harder for you in your life? Is it promoting peace or patiently waiting?
2. What is God challenging you with as you read through this chapter about God's sovereignty in His timing?
3. How have you experienced the satisfying peace of God in your life?
4. Who are some people in your life who would welcome the peace of the Gospel in their life right now?
5. What other ways could you apply these two aspects of the Gospel to your life?

Jonathan Kyle

Chapter 7:

Gospel Living: Endurance, Holiness, and Joy

"We are not the reason the gospel works; the gospel is the reason the gospel works."
Ligon Duncan[35]

Confession, I am a very competitive person. Or I should say I WAS a very competitive person (those close to me may disagree on it being past tense). People who are not competitive do not understand how people like me can get so aggressive and

---

[35] Thabiti Anyabwile, "Blogs: Thabiti Anyabwile," *The Reason the Gospel Works*, February 23, 2011, https://www.thegospelcoalition.org/blogs/thabiti-anyabwile/the-reason-the-gospel-works/

Jonathan Kyle

upset when I lose a game of checkers, UNO, or a backyard game of whiffle ball. All I can say is that no matter what I am playing, it is going to get my very best and, at the very least, every bit of aggressiveness that I have. Competitive people, like myself, cannot understand how someone can play a game and NOT care.

Also, I love tests! In school, I dreaded papers but enjoyed the tests. I loved the simplicity of taking a test and then evaluating where I stood in regards to mastering the content. Combine my competitiveness and my love of tests and you will understand that when I play pick-up games in the backyard, I stack the other team against my own team. First, it allows me to play with full aggressiveness to win the game. Second, I love the challenge that it provides which I know pulls out the best of me and will demand the very best of my teammates. Third, victory is a rewarding accomplishment in the end when you had to overcome so many obstacles. Therefore, when I am stacking the team against myself, I am envisioning the sweetness of the victory on the other side of the game when my team wins. But let's hold all of this in perspective, this is a backyard sport, and I am a washed-up high school athlete, who is out of shape, and way better in my mind than I actually am. That means I greatly respect the professional athlete who carries this mindset into their sport and the ability to still win.

Gospel Living

Recently, I have been watching a documentary on Michael Jordan and the historical run his 90's Bulls team had. While the younger generation may debate whether or not MJ was the greatest professional basketball player ever to play, there is no question for those who grew up watching MJ shred elite defensive players and single-handedly will his comparatively subpar teams to not just victories but championships. Michael Jordan not only transcended the game of basketball in his era but also the world-wide pop culture. Even early in his career while playing against a team with multiple hall of famers, MJ was set apart from those pros by scoring 58 points in the first game. In the second game, he scored what is still a single game playoff record 63 points. Both of these accomplishments were in a losing effort. His performance gained him the most valuable player in both games even though his team lost.

Listen to Michael Jordan speak and it becomes apparent that he is never okay with losing and he will do whatever it takes on the court to win-no matter what it costs him or how much it hurts. Multiple times in his career he played with injuries, but one game stands out as a testament to his willingness to endure difficulty for the satisfaction of a win. With the NBA championship hanging in the balance in a pivotal game 5 in 1997, MJ had the flu. After falling behind by 16 points to the Utah Jazz in the first quarter, a physically exhausted MJ scored 38 points and led the Bull to a two-point victory. Physically drained Jordan was held up by Scottie Pippen to walk off the court.[36]

Why all of this sports history about Michael Jordan, of whom I was not even a fan? Michael Jordan, in the game of professional basketball, was set apart from every other player. He endured great difficulties to accomplish great feats, and he did it all for the satisfaction of a temporal victory. On a much grander scale, the Gospel of Jesus Christ contains the elements of endurance, holiness, and unspeakable joy. Jesus demonstrated these three elements in their fullest. He did this to give His disciples then and today the power to walk the earth with endurance all for the joy that Jesus has gained for them.

Positional and In Progress

I explored this reality of holiness in the first chapter in regards to how Jesus Christ was the perfect sacrifice in order to pay for the sins of mankind, so let me be brief in clarifying what holiness is and how the holiness of Jesus Christ in the Gospel has gained for us positional holiness and

---

[36] Aaron Dodson, June 11, 2017 *On This Day in the NBA Finals History: Michael Jordan's 'Flu Game,'* https://theundefeated.com/features/nba-finals-history-michael-jordan-flu-game/ 4/23/20

empowers us to press on in holiness while we live on this earth. I recommend Jerry Bridges' classic book entitled *The Pursuit of Holiness* for more study on holiness and how a follower of Christ should progress in holiness. Bridges defines holy as "to be morally blameless." Therefore, holiness would imply "separation to God, and the conduct [appropriate to] those so separated."[37]

    Both in the Old Testament and in the New Testament there are two blatant commands for the people of God to be "holy, for I the Lord am holy." In the Old Testament, God gives the command for Moses to speak to Israel as Moses is dictating the Law to God's special people, *"Speak to all the congregation of the people of Israel and say to them, 'You shall be holy, for I the Lord am Holy'"* (Leviticus 19:2). The subsequent giving of the Law and the expectation of them obeying the Law was to set them apart from the rest of the people of the earth and to give them the expectation of what holiness looks like IF they could keep all of the Law. In the New Testament, Peter is encouraging his audience not to be *"conformed to the passions of [their] former ignorance."* Peter challenges the followers of Jesus by saying, *"as he who called you is holy, you also be holy in all your conduct…"* and he quotes the

---

[37] Jerry Bridges, *The Pursuit of Holiness*, (Colorado Springs, CO: NavPress, 2006), pg. 14.

Leviticus passage saying "*...You shall be holy, for I am holy*" (1 Peter 1:14-16). The expectation is clear for Jesus' followers to be set apart and pure, but how does holiness flesh itself out in the Gospel?

Looking back at the 2 Corinthians 5:21 passage, one can read how a person gains a position of holiness before God; "*For our sake he made him to be sin, so that in him we might become the righteousness of God.*" Quickly, one can learn that just as God put the sins of mankind upon Jesus on the cross, now the righteousness (moral excellence) of Christ has been given to those who believe and now are declared to be right with God. In order to be declared righteous before God means that a person is without sin and is holy before Him. This is not a holiness earned by their own ability but given by grace through faith in Jesus. Therefore, followers of Christ have been given positional holiness before God through the work of Jesus Christ on the cross and His resurrection. Through faith in Jesus Christ, one is forgiven of their past, present, and future sins because of His payment on the cross. Therefore, when God looks at His adopted child, He sees the blood of Jesus.

An honest evaluation of oneself, will lead to the discovery that one's actions on this earth and in this flesh are still sinful. Paul gives a great explanation of this in Romans 8. Paul declares that those who are in Christ no longer are condemned for their sin.

Gospel Living

Therefore, a follower of Christ no longer lives to please the sinful desires of their flesh but lives to please the Spirit who lives inside of them. Paul makes it clear that the believer is no longer *"in the flesh but in the Spirit"* because the Spirit dwells inside of them. The beautiful promise in this is found in verses 10-11 that says, *"But if Christ is in you, although the body is dead because of sin, the Spirit is life because of righteousness. If the Spirit of Him who raised Jesus from the dead dwells in you, He who raised Christ Jesus from the dead will also give life to your mortal bodies through His Spirit who dwells in you."* From this text, the believer realizes that their mortal body is dead and implies that their body will struggle with the things of the flesh, but there is coming a day when that body will be resurrected and made alive.

Paul continues in this passage and says, *"So then brothers, we are debtors, not to the flesh, to live according to the flesh"* (12). The disciple of Jesus Christ is not to live chasing after the sinful desires of their mortal flesh. They have been made a new creation that is to seek after the things of God which are righteous. Move over to the book of Philippians and turn to chapter 3, and one can hear this struggle that Paul says the follower of Jesus will have while living in this flesh. Philippians 3:12 says, *"Not that I have already obtained this or am already perfect..."* The "this" Paul is referencing is the "resurrection of the dead" found in verse 11, which he explained in Romans 8. Paul is saying that while he is positionally "holy" before God, in his flesh he has NOT obtained "holiness" in the flesh yet. Does that mean Paul is content in his sin and the position that Christ has granted him before God? NO!! Paul continues in verse 12 by saying, *"...but I press on to make IT my own, because Christ Jesus has made me his own."* Paul emphasizes his need to keep enduring or persevering in this life to live in such a way that separates him from this world and sets him apart as belonging to God. This means there is a balance that a disciple of Christ must always hold in their life of works and faith. They must know their salvation is through faith, but there is a responsibility they have of working and disciplining themselves to grow in holiness by putting to death sin. One must progress in holiness while they are living on this earth and embrace the reality Paul mentions in Philippians 1:6 that says, *"And I am sure of this, that he who began a good wok in you will bring it to completion at the day of Jesus Christ."* As long as you are living, you are in process and not a finished product. How does God grow us in holiness and how does that connect to the Gospel?

Endurance Through Trials Produces Holiness

James opens his letter *"To the twelve tribes in the Dispersion..."* The word

Gospel Living

Dispersion lets the reader know that these are Jewish Christians scattered throughout the region due to persecution. It's safe to say that these followers of Jesus are not in a comfortable spot in their lives. They are probably dealing with a lot of potential anxiety as it pertains to their current and future provision. James' first words to his readers are not what you would expect. James 1:2-4 says, "*Count it all JOY, my brothers, when you meet trials of various kinds, for you know that the testing of your faith produces steadfastness. And let steadfastness have its full effect, that you may be perfect and complete lacking in nothing.*" James tells them that they should rejoice over the fact that they are being tested in many different ways. The tests in their lives and their steadfastness or endurance in it will produce a desired outcome of being made perfect, complete, or mature.

James is saying that if one is steadfast meaning they patiently endure or remain[38] under the trial, they will grow in holiness. This word steadfast or endurance carries with it this idea of faithfully walking in obedience because of one's trust in God that through the trial He is using it to produce something good in them. Believers must be willing to embrace trials and tests in their lives and not run from them in order to

---

[38] https://biblehub.com/greek/5281.htm retrieved 4/30/20

progress in holiness. The key ingredient, though, is not merely surviving the trial, but it is remaining faithful in obedience to the will of God spelled out in His Word while in the trial.

This reality can be seen in a brief interaction between Jesus and Peter just after Jesus instituted the new meaning to the elements of the Passover in Luke 22. Jesus looks at His disciples and tells them in verse 32. "*Simon, Simon, behold, Satan demanded to have you, that he might sift you like wheat, but I have prayed for you that your faith MAY NOT FAIL. And when you have turned again, strengthen your brothers."* Jesus alerts Peter to the fact that Satan wants to test him, and Jesus comforts Peter that He is praying for him that his "*faith may not fail."* Now, my idea of not failing here would be that Peter, like Christ who was tempted in the wilderness, would not give into any temptation and sin. However, Jesus' next words are "*And when you have TURNED AGAIN."* Those last two words are how pastors describe repentance. The idea of repentance is that a person "turns away from sin AND turns back to God." There must always be two sides to repentance because turning away from sin alone will most likely lead that person to return to sin again. We must always follow the turning away from sin with a turning back to God. I say all of that about repentance because with Jesus using that concept it must imply that Jesus knows Peter is not going to withstand the test or temptation. That is not a wild guess for me because the next two verses make it clear when Peter responds, *"'Lord, I am ready to go with you both to prison and to death.' Jesus said, 'I tell you, Peter, the rooster will not crow this day, until you deny three times that you know me."*

I am not saying that Jesus is praying for Peter to sin or is okay with Peter sinning. However, Jesus knows that Peter is going to fail the test, so His prayer is that Peter would not let that failure derail him from pressing on in holiness. Jesus prays for Peter's faith not to fail, meaning that Peter would endure through the test; and that even when he fails, he would repent of his sin and turn back to God so that he can "strengthen [his] brothers." One can read John 21:15-19 and see how Jesus reinforces His prayer and encourages Peter to endure in faithfulness by fulfilling the calling God has for him to pastor. Tests and trials are needed in the life of a believer in order for them to grow in holiness. Succinctly, I would say that Jesus endured trials IN holiness and Christ followers endure trials TO holiness. So, how does a disciple stay motivated to endure the trial?

The Motivation of Joy

I am a person who can be consumed with the next project or big event in my life. As a kid I remember living for the next holiday in my life like my birthday, summer break, and Christmas. I would occasionally have smaller celebrations that I would look forward to like the weekend, but for the most part I kept my focus on the next big event and counting down the days till it came. This type of thinking is still a temptation for me today, although I have learned that I need to "be" in each moment of my life that I am living. I need to be intentional with what God has given for me to do now and not miss it because I am looking to the future.

Therefore, when I try to put myself in Jesus' shoes and imagine what it would be like to live a life that I knew would end in a horrific death, I think there would be multiple days where I would live with intense anxiety and paralyzing fear. Now, I know Jesus is God and in no way did He ever sin but I wonder if He pondered that reality in the quiet moments of His life. That may explain why He retreated to be with His Father so often in prayer. Nevertheless, I just wonder what motivates a person to keep moving forward in a life that he knows is going to end in a gruesome death?

The author of Hebrews gives us the answer that allowed Jesus to endure the trial of the cross in order to give us holiness. The context of these verses in chapter 12 is the great examples of faith of well-known people in the bible and other unnamed brothers and sisters in Christ who believed God in faith, "*not having received the things promised, but having seen them and greeted them from afar..."* (11:13). In other words, some of these people of faith died before they saw the fulfillment of the promise of God on this earth but believed it would take place in eternity. In chapter 12, the author says in light of all of these witnesses and examples of faith that have gone before you, *"let us lay aside every weight, and sin which clings so closely, and let us run with endurance the race that is set before us, looking to Jesus, the founder and perfecter of our faith, WHO FOR THE JOY SET BEFORE HIM endured the cross, despising the shame, and is seated at the right hand of the throne of God"* (12:1b-2). The author pleads with his audience to pursue holiness by walking faithfully and obediently while in the trial, which is what I have been sharing so far in this chapter. But what comes next is the motivation for how they are to keep enduring in the trial. The author tells them to look to Jesus as an example of endurance and His motivation for enduring through the trial of the cross.

The motivation of Jesus to endure the cross and despising its shame was the *"the joy that was set before him."* Jesus saw beyond the cross to the joy that would come on the other side of the cross. Namely, He saw the reconciliation of the world to God through the forgiveness of sins through the shedding of His blood. That is what kept Him motivated to endure the cruelty of the cross. Honestly, you and I don't have the ability to see the future so clearly. That means the believer is to trust by faith that there is an eternal home with God where there is no more sin, shame, tears, and pain.

Paul mentions his motivation for pressing on or seeking so ardently after holiness back in the Philippians 3 passage that is similar to Jesus' motivation. In verse 14 he says, "*I press on toward the goal for the PRIZE OF THE UPWARD CALL of God in Christ Jesus.*" The motivation for Paul in pursuing holiness and the motivation for disciples today is the prize of all the fullness of the presence of God granted to them by the work of Jesus Christ. This is the hope that a believer has in faith or "*conviction of things not seen*" that keeps them enduring faithfully in the midst of trial. All of this means that the Gospel gives us the ability to endure through trials of our life because it will produce holiness and the motivation for enduring faithfully in this life because of the prize of the presence of God that has been earned by Christ.

Applying Endurance, Holiness, and Joy to Our Life Until It Becomes a Lifestyle

With the explosion of technology over the last couple of decades, convenience and comfort have now become no longer electives in one's life but rights that every human deserves. That means if anything makes a person uncomfortable, they will just

Gospel Living

remove themselves from the situation to escape dealing with the issue. While that may cause a temporary easement in a person's life, it does cause many to miss out on the opportunity to learn new skills and grow in maturity.

In the Christian life, believers must not be quick to escape difficulties that arise in their lives. Nowhere in Scripture does Jesus promise life will be easy. In fact, a quick read through the Gospels will reveal to the reader that to be a follower of Christ will require one to embrace sacrifice and suffering in their life. Obviously, this does not mean that a Christian should go around seeking opportunities to take unnecessary risks or do things that causes them to unnecessarily suffer. However, the explicit expectations that Christ gives to His followers are difficult to practice, such as loving one's enemies, being wrong and forgiving that person, and confronting someone that you have wronged in order to seek reconciliation. Not to mention the expectation that disciples would seek to share the Gospel in unreached locations that are hostile to the Gospel, and other holy living that will set apart a Christian from the rest of the world. There are not many people who willingly sign up for that unless they are properly motivated out of love and appreciation for God in which the Gospel has provided for them.

My encouragement is that disciples of Jesus embrace the trials and tests in their lives instead of escaping them. Like lifting weights tears the muscle tissue down only to heal and grow stronger, the only way for a person's faith muscle to grow is by going through the trial trusting in faith that God is going to mature them through the process. The next time a trial comes your way, pause, and see the trial for more than what is currently in front of you. Remember Christ and His willingness to endure the cross because of the joy that would come on the other side of it and declare your dependence upon God by faithfully and obediently walking in His ways during the trial knowing He will perfect you in the journey. The struggles and trials in our lives make the hope of eternity and the presence of God that much sweeter. Matt Chandler in reflecting on the past 10 years of his life during a message at the Village Church gave some lessons that he learned while dealing with the uncertainty of recovery from having a brain tumor removed. He said, "There is nothing we are enduring now that will seem overwhelming 10,000 years from now."[39] This is an incredible thought. In our current fraction of eternity, we deal with so many struggles that seem unsurmountable. However, our perspective looking back will allows us to see

---

[39] Matt Chandler, *Lessons from the Precipice* (December 2nd, 2019)

what those trials produced in our lives and how they allowed us to taste more fully the sweetness of eternity with God.

The other challenge that I give to you is to walk in obedience to the clear commands of God as you walk through the trial. I am often tempted to compromise in obedience when things are getting tough. I experience this a lot in what is for me a lifelong struggle with weight. If things get stressful in my life or I have just had a bad day, I find myself breaking the discipline that I have been practicing and compromise with overindulgence in a sweet treat. I justify in my mind that I deserve this treat because of the day I have had. In the same way, a trial in our life may cause us to wrestle with compromise. We may seek to justify sin in our lives because of how hard things are. Remember, the Gospel empowers us with the ability to say "no" to sin, endure the trial and trust that God will be good on His word and provide the necessary blessings in our lives at just the time we need it. All He asks of us is just to trust and obey. Will you commit to being faithfully obedient to His word and not compromising with sin just because things are currently difficult?

Setting the prize of the presence of God before you in Heaven will serve as the necessary motivation in your life to endure. Undoubtedly, there will be temporary moments of failure where we will give into temptation and sin in the midst of trials.

However, remember that failure is not that we sin but that we do not walk in repentance after we sin. That means if we sin 100 times in a row, we must be steadfast to repent 100 times, each time turning back to Christ. This is a lifelong journey that we are on, and we must keep the bigger picture in our mind and keep pressing on even after temporarily failing. If you are currently in a stage of frequent sin in the midst of trials, do not give up but keep returning to the Lord for forgiveness and submitting your life to His ways. While this ongoing struggle may seem exhausting, we must trust that God is building up your faith muscle to reach a point in the future where your current sin habit will be less of a struggle and provide a testimony for you to speak of the magnificent grace of God and give Him glory.

Living Out the Gospel Questions
1. What is your typical response to trials and tests in your life? What, if anything, needs to change?
2. How does having a bigger picture perspective change the way you view the trials of life and help you through them?
3. How are you going to face the next test and trial of your life differently?
4. What is the one truth that you are going to take out of this chapter and seek to apply to your life?

Gospel Living

Concluding Thoughts

"If you believe what you like in the gospel, and reject what you don't like, it is not the gospel you believe, but yourself."
Augustine[40]

I hope that this book has allowed you to begin to see the robust nature of the Gospel and how the Good News should affect our lives. Even with the characteristics of the Gospel that were discussed in this book there are ample more characteristics of the Gospel that could be expounded on to inspire transformation in the believer's life.

The bottom line is that God has set those who have received the Gospel apart from the rest of the world. We should be distinct. We should be peculiar because we live as aliens and strangers or as "sojourners

---

[40] Erik Raymond, "Blogs: Erik Raymond," *Gospel Quotes*, May 20, 2006   https://www.thegospelcoalition.org/blogs/erik-raymond/gospel-quotes/,

and exiles" in this world. Peter does a great job at proving this point in the second chapter of 1 Peter. Peter calls for his audience to GROW UP! He tells them to put away certain sinful behavior that they used to be a part of and *"Like newborn infants, long for the pure spiritual milk, that by it you may GROW UP into salvation—if indeed you have tasted that the Lord is good"* (2:2-3).

I appreciate these direct and stern watershed statements of Scripture that should cause people who call themselves "Christians" to evaluate whether or not they are true to the nomenclature they give themselves. In essence, Peter is saying that someone who has received the Good News will long more and more for the Word of God in order to apply it to their life and be transformed into something completely other than what they were before. The Christian life is an ongoing process that as believers we should never grow tired of the endless refining of our Savior through His Word as long as we walk this earth.

in verse 3, Peter gives the conditional statement of why someone would progress in their faith. They would progress only if they were truly grateful for the Word and the Gospel that saved them. I want to encourage you to reflect often on the power of the Gospel in your life and out of gratitude, thanksgiving, and love for your Savior that you would relentlessly pursue Him and be malleable to His way for your life.

Jonathan Kyle

In conclusion, I am always amazed at God's Word and how a familiar text that we have read can become more robust over night as we contemplate these truths more and more. I mentioned my favorite verse in the introduction, James 1:22 that says, ""*Do not merely listen to the word, and so deceive yourselves. Do what it says*" (NIV). For a decade I have interpreted "the word" in that verse to be the Bible. In all fairness, that is not a heretical interpretation as there are other Scriptures in the Bible that would support the need for all believers to not just read God's Word but do what it says. However, I recently prepared a message over that verse and asked myself the question, "what is 'the word' that James is referencing?" In verses 17-18, James says ""*Every good gift and every perfect gift is from above, coming down from the Father of lights with whom there is no variation or shadow due to change. Of his own will he brought us forth by the WORD OF TRUTH* (emphasis mine), *that we should be a kind of first fruits of his creatures.*" While we understand that God is the giver of "every perfect gift" that comes into our lives, we know that the greatest gift is Jesus Christ who came from above. James says to the believers that they have been "*brought…forth by the WORD OF TRUTH.*" And this "word" has made them a "first fruit" or a new creation out of His creation. That language is very similar to how Paul describes Jesus' resurrection in 1 Corinthians 15:20 when he says, *"But in fact Christ has been raised from the dead, the FIRSTFRUITS (emphasis mine) of those who have fallen asleep."* It is clear from this passage of Scripture and elsewhere that the "first fruits" language is new life or salvific language.

Hold on to verse 18 in James 1 and move down to verse 21 that says, *"Therefore put away all filthiness and rampant wickedness and receive with meekness the implanted WORD (emphasis mine), which is able to save your souls."* There it is again, "word" and what does it have the capability of doing? This *"word…is able to save your soul…"* Once again, we have salvific language used to describe the "word." This means in James 1 up until this point the "word" is a reference to the Gospel. James 1:22 could then read *"Do not merely listen to the Gospel, and so deceive yourselves. Respond to it and let it change who you are"* (my translation).

James goes on to use an illustration of a mirror and how foolish it would be to look into a mirror, go away, and immediately forget what you look like. He likens this kind of foolishness to the one who hears the Gospel message or "the word" and does not do it. In a Gospel sense, foolish is the person who is confronted with the reality of who God is and the sinfulness of their own condition, and the solution of for their sin in the work of

Jesus Christ, yet they refuse to respond or do anything about it. However, the person is blessed *"who looks into the perfect law, the law of liberty, and perseveres, being no hearer who forgets but a doer who acts..."* Notably, they are blessed in being granted forgiveness and receiving eternal life. Generally, the person who submits themselves to the Lordship of Jesus Christ and His commands will find it keeps them out of trouble and helps them navigate successfully through this world.

With this understanding, the consistent pattern of a believer's life is to open up the perfect mirror of God's Word on a daily basis and evaluate themselves and make the appropriate course corrections to their life, so they can line up with the Bible or with the Gospel. As long as you are living, these facets of the Gospel are to be admired, understood, and applied to your life. Do not settle for anything less than the standard of perfection, holiness. That means, as long as you are living, you should always be growing.

As much as I want you to be inspired to go out and look for ways to apply these truths to your life, I want you to first take a good long look at the Gospel. You must understand its implications in your life, and, out of amazement and love for your Wonderful God, strive daily to live changed by the Gospel that has saved you. Live like your Savior!

Gospel Living

Jonathan Kyle

Author's Biography

Jonathan is the Copastor and Student Pastor at Candies Creek Baptist Church in Cleveland, Tennessee. He has served in the ministry for over 15 years as a Student Pastor and has a real gift of bridging the gap between doctrine and practice. This stems from his passion of applying God's Word to life until it becomes a lifestyle. He is married to his wife, Amanda, and has four kids.

Jonathan Kyle

Gospel Living

Made in United States
Orlando, FL
21 February 2022

15032519R00102